Hollywood Victory Caravan

I. Joseph Hyatt

Hollywood Victory Caravan

A pictorial history of America's largest bond drive.

To purchase books in quantity for fund raising or incentives email HVCScrapbook@aol.com.

ISBN: 1514240874
ISBN 13: 978-1514240878

DEDICATION

Veteran - *noun* \'ve-ta-ran, 've tran\ - A veteran is someone who, at one point in his life, wrote a blank check made payable to "The United States of America" for an amount of "up to and including my life."

This book is dedicated to my father, Technician Fifth Grade I. J. Hyatt of the US Army who was wounded during World War Two in the European Theater, released from service, and lived until 1982. He was survived by 2 children.

This book is dedicated to Sergeant J. J. Lavin of the US Army Air Corp, who served during World War Two in the Asiatic-Pacific Theater. A B-29 machine gunner, he was "mustered" out after the war was over. He lived until October 2013, days before this book was finished. He was survived by 7 children, 14 grandchildren, and 2 great-grandchildren.

This book is also dedicated to all that served fighting for their country's freedom, and for the lives we enjoy today. We owe a debt that can never be repaid to these military men, both US and Allied forces.

Finally this book is dedicated to the residents and staff of the Menlo Park Veteran's Home, in Edison, New Jersey. The "all for one and one for all" style that permeated our culture during the Second World War, and flows throughout the pages of this book are still a large part of their daily lives. God Bless and keep these people well for their service and sacrifices. Thank you.

ACKNOWLEDGEMENTS

A large thanks goes to my wife, Mary, who must have sat through more than a year listing to my oral readings of this book. Hers is always the correct decision. Thank you to Lois Laurel-Hawes, who again supplied material for this book. Michael Ehret supplied most of the Mexican material, as well as other rare photos. Ron Hutchenson, who helped provide some of the material that brings the human element into the story.

Roger Robinson, Chris Coffey, Randy Skretvedt, Scott MacGillivray, Glenn Mitchell, Roger Gordon, John Ullah, Willie McIntyre, Antony and Joanne Mitchell-White, Dave Heath (and his Another Fine Mess website), Bill and Savannah Furman, and those who have added to our knowledge base by their fine books, articles, and newsletters.

Friends whose hands pushed this project along over the last 30+years included Russell Clay, Adrian Brailsford, Dave Newton, Ruth Newton, "Mad" Paul Allen, Cliff Sawyer, Gino Dercola, and Dwain Smith.

Mark, PJ, Gerry, and Brielle Eisler, who are family to me. Perry Smith, Dell Kempster, David Dearle, Rene Riva, Jeffery Holland, Andreas Baum, and Bill Duelly.

The Union Country Performing Arts Center, its staff and fundraising group, Friends of the Union County Arts Center. The theater was built in 1928, and, with its original Wurlitzer 2/7 organ, they help keep our celluloid history visible.

Carl and Julie Mintzer - thanks for the proof reading of this manuscript. I still take the blame for whatever typing and language errors exist. Julie told me to do a final re-write, but I thought a photo copy would be sufficient.

As always, I can't forget departed friends Bill Cubin, original founder of the Laurel and Hardy Museum in Ulverston, England, "Happy" Harry Ingle, Dougie Rimmer, and my good friend Jimmy Murphy.

I. JOSEPH HYATT

CONTENTS

Dedication and Acknowledgments iii

INTRODUCTION

This book is a Scrapbook of the Hollywood Victory Caravan, a three-week journey in April - May of 1942 that brought a number of famous performers across the United States to raise money for The Army and Navy Relief Society. Funded by civilians except for time of war, these charities were created for the families and children of the military during their time of need.

Original Staff Collar Badge - Worn above left and right collar points when in uniform.

The Hollywood Victory Caravan was the greatest public relations piece that the Motion Picture industry had ever produced. The show itself turned in more money to the Army and Navy Relief Funds than any other single effort up to that date.

It was estimated that with the parades, performances, hotel appearances, etc. that crowds of over 8,000,000 saw the performers, with only a fraction of these able to actually see the shows. In Washington, D.C. their appearance at the White House helped with the morale of over hundreds of thousands of tired war workers, civilians and military personnel.

In Boston alone there were an estimated million people who stood just to get a glimpse of the stars along a parade route that gave maximum exposure to as many viewers as possible. That evening, the Hollywood Victory Caravan played to more people than have ever been gathered under one roof.

In Chicago, the gross receipts tripled any stage attraction ever seen. In St. Paul, the one evening performance doubled any show that appeared in that city for a full week's stand. The show in Des Moines the crowd was larger than any planned gathering. Until the Hollywood Victory Caravan arrived, the largest gathering had been Army Day at 106,000. The parade was before 360,000 people. Nickels and dimes collected during the parade totaled over $4000.00.

In Philadelphia, Cleveland, Detroit, St. Louis, Minneapolis, Dallas and Houston, more people were gathered together than for any event before, including the Armistice for World War One.

Columnists Louella Parsons and Paul Harrison were permitted to see some early rehearsals at Paramount Studios, who graciously donated space to the Caravan. Paul Harrison was greatly impressed by the effort and reported so in his column of May 1, 1942:

"As one who hung around watching the show being put together, I can tell you that the spirit and effort was like nothing ever seen in this region of temperament, pride and ease. They worked themselves to a frazzle and enjoyed it. They took direction meekly. They served as mere stooges in acts starring other players. Dignity was kicked out the window as they kidded themselves and Hollywood.

"Even before they left Hollywood, Frank McHugh was black and blue from the violence of a first-aid demonstration practiced on him by the normally charming and gentle Claudette Colbert. I don't know what she'll wear on the tour, but it was quite a sight at a rehearsal when the actress, in a too-tight skirt, planted a foot on his chest to tighten bandages or struggled to give him artificial respiration."

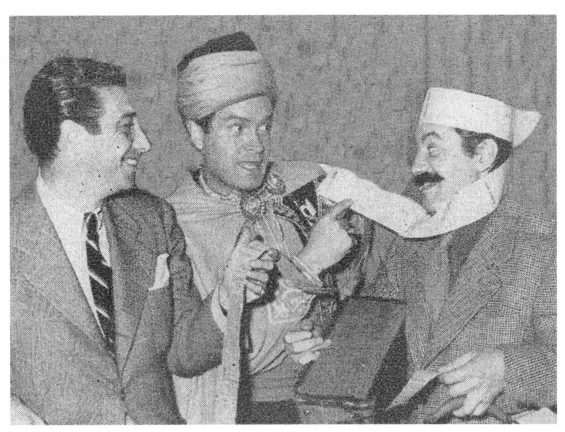

Mark Sandwich watches as Bob Hope (in uniform from his film "Road To Morocco") and Jerry Colonna examine the length of their train ticket. Here Hope points to Houston, Texas, the last scheduled stop of the Hollywood Victory Caravan. Photo taken at Paramount Studios.

Merle Oberon, Joan Blondell and Joan Bennett dismantle an engine in a rehearsal of "The Ladies" on the Paramount lot.

Most performers stayed with the show throughout its entire journey. Others joined or left as their schedules permitted and obligations allowed. Before the opening of the first show, members of the Caravan were received by Eleanor Roosevelt at the White House on the afternoon of April 30, 1942.

This book represents 40 years of research that involved cross country travel to archives and personal collections. It contains photographs, and interviews with people who saw the show, and quotes from some of those who participated in the events connected to the presentations. Most of the material was gathered by actually retracing the tour route personally (during those pre-internet days).

Some items, like the original national press book, were retyped due to the brittleness of the original, keeping many of the original typos and errors intact. There were possibly 150 - 200 of these printed originally and distributed to the newspapers in the cities where the Caravan performed. Most of these were disposed of immediately after the event. In years of collecting, this is the only one I've ever found. Letters and newspaper clippings were also cleaned up and reproduced as clearly as possible.

Autographed and inscribed photos to Oliver "Babe" Hardy and Bob Hope were reprinted from each star's own souvenir program. These are of the originals, as signed by the stars who were on the tour..

I hope the "Hollywood Victory Caravan Scrapbook" brings back the feeling and experience that everyone must have felt back in the 1940's when the country all pulled together for a common goal.

The "Star Spangled Special" at Union Station leaving for Washington, DC. on April 26, 1942.

On the platform on April 26 at Los Angeles: Frances Langford, Pat O'Brien, Rise Stevens, Joan Blondell, Faye MacKenzie, Arleen Whelan, Desi Arnaz, Eleanor Powell, Mark Sandrich (producer), Charlotte Greenwood and Frank McHugh. On the ground: Charles Boyer, Jerry Colonna, Bert Lahr, Cary Grant, Frances Gifford, Marie McDonald, Ray Middleton, Bette Davis, Oliver Hardy, Stan Laurel and Elyse Knox. Saying farewell on their way east. In the background are the soldiers and sailors who formed an honor guard as the company left. Stars not pictured would catch up with the tour by plane for the first show on April 29.

Uniform patch worn by Camp Shows employees.

IN THE BEGINNING.....

The USO (United Service Organizations, Inc.) was formed in 1941 to aid in the war and defense program of the United States and its Allies by serving the religious, spiritual, welfare, and educational needs of the men and women in the armed forces and the war defense industries and to contribute to the morale in American communities and elsewhere.

Hollywood and its stars and crews were eager to show support and patriotism for their country. Many famous celebrities joined the ranks of USO entertainers, without recompense. They entertained in military bases at home and overseas, sometimes placing their own lives in danger, by traveling or performing under hazardous conditions. They also worked in the USO Canteens that were located across the US. Stars did everything from mingle and perform, to washing dishes and serving food.

Original poster from a "Camp Shows" performance at a base service club.

Affiliated and supported by the USO, a separate group, Camp Shows Incorporated, was put together to coordinate all this entertainment for the United States and Allied service men overseas, at home, in hospitals, in occupied territories, and for civilian bond drives. They made contact with Hollywood booking agents, producers, writers, music arrangers, musicians and other notables to lend a hand and donate their services. Camp Shows Incorporated was also created to "ration" the stars and gain maximum impact for their time invested.

WWII USO Camp Shows window sticker that was displayed only at USO locations presenting USO Camp Show events.

The Hollywood Victory Caravan show was partially inspired by an all-star bond show at Madison Square Garden on March 10, 1942. Done for Navy Relief, organized by Walter Winchell, the newspaper columnist., the show proved that many stars could bring in many donations and much publicity.

The original Madison Square Garden Navy Releif all-star show initially conceived and principally produced by Walter Winchell, March 10, 1942. This one show raised over $160,000 and was one of several Winchel was involved in. These shows included many major cities, including Miami and San Francisco. Along with these one of a kind variety shows, Winchell also did many boxing exibitions to draw in more cash for Navy Relief.

Some of the original performers were Bette Davis, Tyrone Powers, and Kate Smith.

Original McClelland Barclay poster for Winchell's Madison Square Garden Show. Barclay was a famous "pin-up" artist in the 1930's. Serving in the Navy as a Lt. Commander, Barclay was reported missing in action on July 18, 1943 after his ship was torpedoed in the Solomon Islands.

The next precursor to the actual Hollywood Victory Caravan Tour took place at the Teatro Mayan, in Ensenada, Mexico. On March 21, 1942 a group of 132 troupers traveled over 200 miles by special train to San Diago, where the Caravan had a night's sleep. The next morning everyone boarded four busses and, along with a carload with the costumes, and sound and lighting equipment. Traveling over mountains, and on dirt roads to the Lower California Mexican military headquarters. Special diplomatic arrangements were made for the border and immigration passing. The Caravan was accompanied from the border by American and Mexican motorcycle escort. They were greeted by Lieutenant Asner Zertina of the Mexican Navy, who welcomed them on behalf of President Avila Camacho and the Mexican Government. Lieutenant Zertina said that "the sincere friendship of the United States is evidenced by Hollywood sending to Mexico as big a show as has gone out to any of its own Army camps." The fifty actual performers performed a four hour show in the theater, on the Main Street in Ensenada in front of 2500 Mexican soldiers and sailors and the majority of the town..

The Teatro Maya located on Ensenada's Main Street in Mexico.

Among the performers were some who became involved in the 12 city Caravan tour in the US. Those who performed were Jimmy Cagney, Dick Powell, Joan Blondell, Joan Bennett, Desi Arnaz, Stan Laurel and Oliver Hardy. Additional performers included Ann Miller, Lucille Ball, the Merry Macs, Mary Martin, and the famous songwriter Irving Berlin.

After Pearl Harbor, there was a concern that Japan might attack Mexico to use as a base for its war against the USA. During this period of the war, the US and Mexico became partners in the west coast defense. This show was to bring up the morale of the fighting men, and to help cement relations.

This expedition was a combination production of the Motion-Picture Society for the Americas, which was a section of the Rockefeller Latin-American relations committee, and the Hollywood Victory Committee for Stage, Screen, and Radio. All the expenses were covered by the Motion-Picture Society while stars (all volunteer) were arranged by the Hollywood Victory Committee. It was a good partnership.

An audio recording of the entire show was recorded, and played at many Mexican bases.

The original cast for the Ensenada show poses for a photograph in Mexico. Visible are Cary Grant, Desi Arnaz, Dick Powell, Joan Blondell, Jimmy Cagney, Ann Miller, Stan Laurel and many more.

Oliver Hardy examines Lupe Valez's foot. Was it his misstep that created the injury?

Laurel and Hardy posing with some of the starlets who performed that day for newspaper publicity.

Another publicity photo with Laurel and Hardy.

Laurel and Hardy perform their Driver's License Sketch on the Teatro Maya stage in front of an American and Mexican flag display.

It was shortly after this that solid plans for the Hollywood Victory Caravan were made. The Hollywood Victory Caravan, as a patriotic gesture from America's entertainment industry, was a great boost to America's home front morale. Nothing was rationed for what was to be America's largest bond drive. While the Caravan missed its monetary target by a bit, it focused the country's attention on the families of servicemen and their needs. For this reason, the effort was priceless.

The Hollywood Victory Caravan tour was originally set to have had more stars. By the 23rd of April it was announced that Irene Dunn, Mary Martin, Victor Mature, Norma Shearer, Hedy Lamarr, Ann Sheridan, Edward Arnold, and Errol Flynn were also joining the group. Prior commitments could not be cleared, and prevented them all from participating.

MR. SPENCER TRACY

Spencer Tracy did not appear with the Hollywood Victory Caravan. The Washington, D.C. souvenir program was printed with his photo and credit while his name actually appeared in many newspaper ads.

Just a few days before the show was scheduled to start Spencer Tracy also had to cancel. Some cities had the programs and ads already printed and prepared before his cancelation occurred. You will see him mentioned as appearing on and off throughout the material reproduced in this book, but he never joined the Caravan.

Mark Sandwich, the show's producer, was best known for being a musical-comedy director and producer in Hollywood. His directing credits included Bert Wheeler and Robert Woolsey films, as well as Fred Astaire and Ginger Rogers movies. Succeeding as a director, he moved up to take the role of producer for two successful Jack Benny pictures, and also the Bing Crosby and Fred Astaire's perennial Christmas classic "Holiday Inn".

Sandrich used an innovative approach for the time in this live production. He had a telephone backstage connected with the conductor, cast and the operator of the lights, so he could edit the show as it went along to keep it in tune with the audience reaction. It was possible to switch any routine, or change it, in the midst of the show, a necessity based on venue and availability of the artists.

Sandrich's choice of participants showed a sharp awareness of the mix needed for a three hour show. Many of the stars had roots in stage and vaudeville, and were right at home doing live performances. Laurel and Hardy had just come out of doing a live tour. Cagney, Colbert, O'Brien, Lahr and Greenwood all had impressive stage credentials, and were a great help to the starlets and actors who were new to the footlights.

When interviewed after the show, Sandrich recounted: "Camp Shows, Inc. had handed me a list of talent.," he said. "Here y'are, m'boy. Make something of this." His normal tradition of higher budget productions had been shattered by this assignment. "I'll never be the same again. Hollywood's super-specials will look like 'shoe string' productions after this!" The estimated cost of the talent gathered was over four million dollars (in 1942 dollars)!

The co-operative effort that went into the whole production underscores the patriotism existing in America. Hotels in each city donated rooms for the troupe. The Santa Fe Railroad donated the use of the train that was named "Star Spangled Special". By Federal law, the cost of the actual use of the tracks had to be paid for out of the proceeds, but few other costs were incurred to lower the money that went to the cause.

Mark Sandrich

Alfred Newman

The train consisted of ten to fourteen railroad cars, depending on what cities were traveled between. These cars contained sleeping compartments, separated by sex and chaperoned, and dining rooms and common bar cars, where the stars entertained each other when they were not rehearsing. For rehearsals "on board" there were two portable dance floors, two pianos and ten musicians as well. On train rehearsals were referred to as "mile-a-minute rehearsals" by the press. Alfred Newman, the music director augmented his orchestra with local musicians in each city. The total "on stage" troupe for opening night consisted of 75 people.

The Writer's Mobilization, headed by Allan Scott, contributed the script for the show. Writers included S.J. Perelman, composers Arthur Schwartz, Johnny Mercer and Frank Loesser.

Many of the day's popular songs were specifically chosen to make it easier for the local musicians to work with the Caravan's traveling musicians. Jerome Kern wrote a new song called "Windmill in the Sky" specifically for the show. Also contributing were Howard Lindsay, George S. Kaufman, Julius and Phillip Epstein, True Boardman, Russell Crouse, Moss Hart, George Oppenheimer, and Matt Brooks.

Some stars, such as Laurel and Hardy needed no new material written for them, they used their "Driver's License Sketch" which proved popular for them during all their public appearances.

Groucho Marx was at a point in his career where he was ready to go as a single. On stage since his days traveling in vaudeville, Groucho had announced his retirement as a Marx Brother. During his time with the Hollywood Victory Caravan he tried to promote himself as the new Groucho Marx. He would be playing as himself, with no black greasepaint and no black frock coat. He had performed new material in a sketch with Olivia de Havilland. He found that he had to revert to his customary make-up for this sketch, just to be recognized. One large city newspaper even referred to him in a photo as his brother, Harpo Marx.

He also had the chance to sing one of his favorite Harry Ruby songs: "I'm Doctor Hackenbush", originally written for the MGM's Marx Brothers film "A Day at the Races." Never used in the movie, it became one of the most popular segments of the Caravan show. Groucho did this in full make-up, including a white doctor's coat.

An unbelievable huge train, large sign, giant cast and a great cause.

Jerry Colonna mugs for the cameraman with Charlotte Greenwood in the background. (Frame enlargement)

Arlene Whelan and Elyse Knox are escorted to the train by a group of sailors. (Frame enlargement)

Cary Grant blows kisses to the photographers behind Rise Stevens. (Frame enlargement)

Bert Lahr brought out his "Woodsman" routine from his stage days. With his trademark voice, sawdust, and even flying logs punctuating the comedy, it was audience tested before it opened.

Charlotte Greenwood reached back decades for songs and comedy that she performed for years in her successful play, "So Long Letty."

The newly written material for Claudette Colbert, Olivia de Havilland, Charles Boyer, and Joan Bennett had a brief rehearsal time at Paramount studios to let them learn their lines before boarding the train. Louella Parsons, the famous Hollywood columnist, kept an eye on the proceedings, and the "insider's knowledge" that she acquired made for good columns and good publicity.

The train also carried essential props, set pieces, and oleos (hand painted backdrops). Popular in vaudeville theatre and still used today, they require a minimum of travel space, and can be hung from any overhead rigging. Changing the background during the show was a simple as "dropping" oleos into place, bringing out the props, and opening the curtains.

Costumes were also transported along with the performers. Eleanor Powell was carrying more than half the costumes she wore in "Ship Ahoy." These outfits were on loan from the MGM studio. She had several more especially created for the Caravan. Like all the other stars, she was always dressed for her public, even when not on stage.

A frame enlargement from 16mm home movie shot in Philadelphia: The oleo of a tree and a prop swing set occupy the stage during the performance of "Where's Olive?" by Olivia de Havilland and Groucho Marx.

An oleo also provided the background of the Bureau of Internal Revenue, behind Cary Grant and Bert Lahr. (Frame enlargement)

The Hollywood Victory Caravan train had an unscheduled stop on the way in the city of Amarillo, Texas Monday, April 27th. Through the windows and on the back platform, while the military and police kept anyone from nearing the train, the performers were happy to receive public attention two days earlier than expected. The reason for the stop? Bert Lahr had to register with the selective service board.

Since he was so busy with preliminary rehearsal, he was unable to register the Saturday before they left. He was given a two-day extension. All male citizens between the ages of 44 to 65 were required to register under the law. for classification of potential usefulness in the war effort. It was doubtful Lahr would have been asked to do anything that would impede him from providing entertainment for the morale, which he did throughout the war. Over 1350 men were registered that afternoon at the Borger, Texas facility. Following Bert Lahr's ceremony, the Santa Fe Railway's Star Spangled Victory train was on its way again.

While on tour, cast members were not allowed to appear in other engagements during the entire run of the tour. One exception was made for Bob Hope's radio broadcast, which had already started broadcasting from military bases. It was felt that his program added to the morale of the troupes. He broadcasted from the Great Lakes Naval Training Station near Waukegan, Illinois, on May 5, 1942. His second broadcast during the Caravan was on May 12 at the Music Hall adjacent to the Houston Coliseum where the Caravan was performing the same night. Both broadcasts were to an almost all-military audience.

That was the plan, however occasionally a star or two (or more) would sneak away, to a hospital, golf match, or other event. Groucho Marx even traveled to Cleveland from Detroit just to heckle his brother Chico who was appearing as a single in a night club. Mark Sandrich's intense lectures about professionalism when they returned seemed to do nothing to stop this practice among the performers that had determination.

Frances Langford, Bob Hope and Jerry Colonna during a live radio broadcast in studio. Note the soundproofing on the wall.

Bob Hope, Frances Langford, Olivia de Havilland, and Jerry Colonna did not travel on the Caravan train, but had to fly into Washington due to radio commitments. Jimmy Cagney also flew in alone from New England, where he was on vacation.

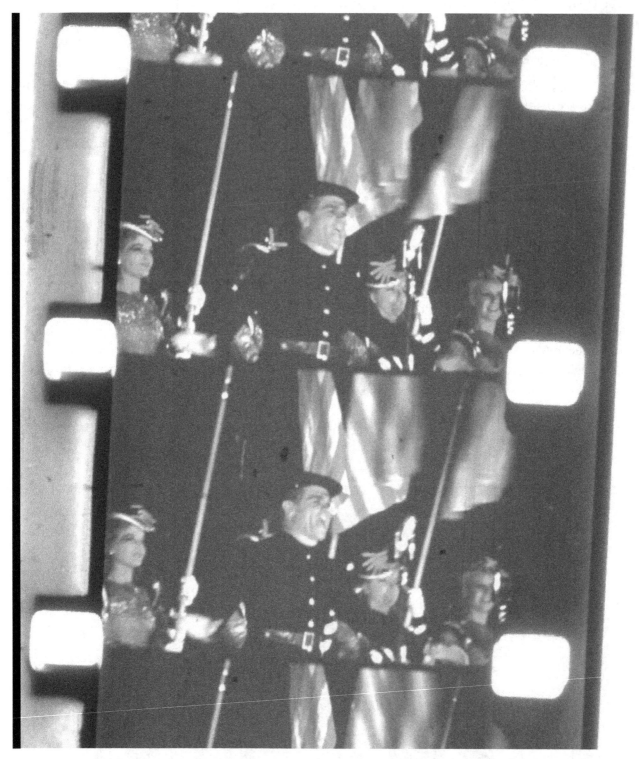

Warner Brothers allowed Jimmy Cagney to do an advance presentation of his dances for the yet unreleased movie "Yankee Doodle Dandy" as his contribution to the Caravan. The costumes worn by Cagney and the starlets for these numbers were the original ones used in the film, and were on loan from Warner Brothers. This is a 1942 film section of a home movie taken of Cagney in full performance.

The train left LA's Union Station on April 26, 1942. Five minutes out of LA, Mark Sandrich called for the first rehearsal to take place. Since the troupe had only two days of rehearsals before boarding, it was important for the team to use every minute they had. They were opening in less than 4 days. Sandrich's rehearsals were for ten hours a day until the train arrived in Washington.

On the day before the actual performance, they had the luxury of a full dress rehearsal in the Loew's Capitol theater which started at midnight and lasted to the early morning hours of the 30th. Few stops would have this much time available before performance times.

The finished product - which changed in every city - was planned to be a three hour show. The first night ran over three-and- one-half hours. Because of this, many of the opening night pieces played that evening only, reducing the length of following shows. The order of these numbers were constantly revised. Variety, the entertainment industry's trade paper, called the Hollywood Victory Caravan "the most distinguished one-night stand company in history."

An ambitious goal of $750,000 was set by the committee. It was hoped that 150,000 people would see the show at an expensive $5.00 a seat. The Committee also hoped to sell boxes at $1000 apiece.

THE WHITE HOUSE
WASHINGTON

April 22, 1942

TO THE HOLLYWOOD VICTORY CARAVAN SHOW:

     Once again the Nation is placed in the debt of the artists who comprise your group for their unselfish efforts to make life easier for the families of our fighting men.

     I like the name you have chosen because it is predicated on the certainty of victory. That is the spirit which will win the war. It gives me great pleasure to extend this assurance of my appreciation to every participant and I am confident the Hollywood Victory Caravan Show will be the rousing success which its high purpose merits.

From Franklyn Delano Roosevelt, 32nd President of the United States 1933-1945.

THE PRESS BOOK

The press book had a card weight cover that was black on green. Due to the war paper shortage and endless paper drives its interior pages were printed on a low-grade soft paper. Now too soft and yellow to reproduce well, the book has been retyped for inclusion, but done in a similar layout and with its pages the same order as in the original.. The typeface was modernized for consistency. The typeface on the first page photo below is typical to the original.

The National Press Book of the Hollywood Victory Caravan.

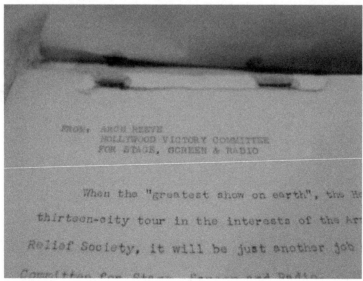

What the newspapers used for publicity and background. Note the one-sided typing paper, stapled at the top. This original documents were printed and circulated just days before the tour.

The rush to get this booklet to the newspapers in time for advance publicity for the Caravan meant that the press book had been put together quickly. Some of the pages in the press book are dated within 8 days of the first performance. Cary Grant did not know he would be a part of this show until the movie he was to do next was postponed so he could appear in the Caravan. He found out on April 23, barely in time to be included in this press book.

A lot of the information on each star contained some odd errors and fabrications as well. As in almost everything Hollywood did, the legend became the fact. When you see an oddity that you recognize as wrong, know in the end these stories gave what the 40's fans wanted, and served the purpose they were designed for - publicity.

Put together by what appears to be separate typists from the individual studios, the last page of the release contains the phrase "23 stars." Spencer Tracy was to have been a part of the Caravan, but he had to cancel. His biography pages and background information were physically removed from each press book before its original distribution. There was no time to change "23" to "22" stars, or Tracy's name so this is how it was distributed.

Photos appearing throughout the press book pages are frame enlargements from a color home movie that was taken on May 2, 1942, at the Philadelphia show. These stills are from the only home movie footage known to exist today of the actual performances. They were not a part of the original press book. The show itself was not professionally filmed, although it had been suggested.

Due to the nature of enlarging 16mm images with movements within each frame, the image appears softer than what comes from an actual still photograph. In a darkened hall, lit for the thousands of patrons, lighting variations created some contrast, brightness, and color issues in the amateur film. For the color edition of this book, color has been corrected to appear as it did to an audience member, subject to the stage lighting. For the black and white version of this book adjustments have also been made to the images. This film, in a private collection, appears to be the only "complete" show to ever be recorded.

Originally shot in color this is a frame enlargement of a 16mm home movie. Laurel and Hardy on stage in Philadelphia. (Frame enlargement)

FROM: ARCH REEVE   FOR IMMEDIATE RELEASE

HOLLYWOOD VICTORY COMMITTEE

FOR STAGE, SCREEN & RADIO

When the "greatest show on earth", the Hollywood Victory Caravan, ends a thirteen-city tour in the interests of the Army Emergency Relief and the Navy Relief Society, it will be just another job completed by the Hollywood Victory Committee for Stage, Screen and Radio.

This organization, formed a few days following our entry into the war, has furnished hundreds of stars and players for thousands of appearances at Army Camps, Naval stations, service benefits and other war-time fund and morale raising activities.

Created as a clearing-house for star activity, it has accomplished the

purpose for which it was established – the control of entertainment talent so that the greatest good could be accomplished for the nation.

Hundreds of requests clear the desks of the Hollywood Victory Committee weekly. Working in close cooperation with government officials, the committee allots this talent in such a manner as to reap the fullest harvest.

The all-important "morale" factor is taken into consideration as the committee studies requests. In many instances it has been considered more important to send a star to a remote military camp to entertain service men than to send the same personality to a more accessible district on a fund raising mission.

The past month has been typical. Screen stars entertained at thirty-three Army and Navy camp shows throughout the country. They took part in seventeen great radio broadcasts that had to do with the war. They attended hundreds of other functions that contributed in some manner to the nation's war task.

Starting June 1st, the Hollywood Victory Committee will send thirty top screen stars to 120 of our largest cities to sell war bonds and stamps, following a request for this activity from the Secretary of the Treasury.

The personnel of the Hollywood Victory Committee represents a cross-section of every phase of the entertainment industry. Hollywood's most successful producers, actors, publicists, writers, directors and agents serve on the committee. Their time is donated, their abilities contributed without cost to writing, acting, casting, directing and managing the many units that are formed each month as one of the motion picture industry's contributions to the national emergency.

- - - - -

424-24

Seven of the starlets start the show with song and interact with Bob Hope, the opening emcee.

All 8 starlets did the back-up singing for Groucho's live performance of the song "Dr. Hackenbush", which was from but not used in "A Day at the Races". (Frame enlargements)

OUTLINE OF PROGRAM MATERIAL FOR
H O L L Y W O O D   V I C T O R Y   C A R A V A N

Sponsor: HOLLYWOOD VICTORY COMMITTEE OF STAGE
SCREEN & RADIO

Producer and Director: MARK SANDRICH

Musical Director: ALFRED NEWMAN

Stars:

DESI ARNEZ	OLIVIA DeHAVILAND
GROUCHO MARX	JOAN BENNETT
CARY GRANT	FRANK McHUGH
JOAN BLONDELL	CHARLOTTE GREENWOOD
RAY MIDDLETON	CHARLES BOYER
BOB HOPE (Master of Ceremonies)	MERLE OBERON
JAMES CAGNEY	PAT O'BRIEN
CLAUDETTE COLBERT	BERT LAHR
ELEANOR POWELL	JERRY COLONNA
FRANCES LANGFORD	RISE STEVENS
	LAUREL & HARDY

Starlets:

KATHERINE BOOTH	MARIE McDONALD
ALMA CARROLL	FAY McKENZIE
FRANCES GIFFORD	JUANITA MSTARK
ELYSE KNOX	ARLEEN WHELAN

DANNY DARE   Dance Ensembles

Writers: Members of the Hollywood Writers' Mobilizations who contributed their time and talents in writing the music, lyrics, skits and dramatic sequences for the Hollywood Victory Caravan are as follows:

ALLAN SCOTT, Chairman

MARTIN BERKELEY	RUSSELL CROUSE
IRVING BRECKER	KEN ENGLUND
MATT BROOKS	MOSS HART
JEROME CHODOROV	GEORGE KAUFMAN
HOWARD LINDSAY	

Special Music and Lyrics by:
JEROME KERN
JOHN MERCER
FRANK LOESSER
ARTHUR SCHWARTZ

Sets designed by: MILT GROSS

Stage Manager – HOWARD DEIGHTON

Production Assistants – ARTHUR JACOBSON
AL FISHER

To me, this Victory Caravan is the best thing yet to come out of Hollywood in the interest of national defense. Sure, we in the picture business buy bonds and make radio appearances and participate in everything else that our nation calls upon us to do, but the Victory Caravan is something else. We want it to be The Greatest Show on Earth because it is the Greatest Cause on Earth. I feel highly honored in being permitted to be a part of it.

Signed (Pat O'Brien)

I am extremely happy to be a part of the Hollywood Victory Caravan and to be doing my bit for the very worthy cause it represents. It enables me to obey the orders of my commanding officers in the Cuban Military Reserve who has just answered my request for active duty with instructions to continue for the present with the work I have been doing on behalf of the USO. I sincerely hope our earnest endeavor will help the Hollywood Caravan attain the goal it has set.

Signed (Desi Arnez)

The player members of the Hollywood Victory Caravan are, I am sure, anticipating more pleasure for themselves than they possibly could give to any audience. The mere fact that our talents can help in any degree the cause of the Army Emergency Relief and Naval Relief Society is to each of us a glowing and heartfelt satisfaction.

It is my sincere hope that our offerings will be received with even a fraction of the pleasure that is ours in the giving."

Signed (Cary Grant)

Out in Hollywood we're planning day and night on forthcoming entertainment programs for our soldiers and sailors. Of course we're working all hours turning out entertaining motion pictures but in between pictures most of the screen players I know are using their vacation periods to entertain in person at the army camps and navy centers.

It's a wonderful treat for us all to get away on the Hollywood Victory Committee Caravan and to feel that we can have a grand time while doing our little bit.

Personally. I'm getting one of the biggest thrills of my life meeting the thousands sailors and soldiers in a dozen big cities on our tour, as well as the public which is contributing so generously to the Army and Navy Relief Fund. ....Joan Bennett

"The Hollywood Victory Caravan, recognizing that heroism does not bloom on the battlefronts alone, but also in the hearts of bereft families left behind, is dedicated to the task of lightening their burdens insofar as it is possible to do so.

It is with great pride that I am privileged to join this worthy and profoundly patriotic cause."

Signed (Ray Middleton)

To be a member of the Hollywood Victory Caravan is, indeed, a great honor and I am proud of the privilege accorded me in being allowed to do my small bit in aiding this great and glorious cause.

Signed (Merle Oberon)

"Every American has a job to do. At the moment my job is entertainment. To be privileged to produce and direct the Hollywood Victory Caravan show, featuring a score of favorite stars, is in itself a great honor, but to me more important is the opportunity to serve in my humble way the furthering of the great Army and Navy Relief Program."

Signed (Mark Sandrich)

"I can't shoulder a rifle but if these machine gun taps of mine can help this magnificent cause in even a small way, I am thrilled to be able to do my share."

Signed (Eleanor Powell)

I consider it an unusual privilege to be associated with the Hollywood Victory Caravan. I have only the highest regard and admiration for its motives. These aims and the enthusiasm and spirit of those involved in this endeavor are so thoroughly and sincerely identified with the national objectives of our great nation that I am sure only the most signal success can mark its efforts.

Signed (Charles Boyer)

Nothing ever done by actors in the history of show business has been as important as this Victory Caravan and I am genuinely proud that I have been asked to be a part of it.

Signed (Claudette Colbert)

This is the single greatest movement of stars in the history of entertainment. I am happy that this is for the benefit of the most beneficial charitable movements I have ever encountered.

Signed (Bob Hope)

"The Hollywood Victory Caravan will prove to be, I hope, a very practical expression of the eagerness of the members of the acting profession to devote their special talents to patriotic service. I consider it a privilege – and I am sure my sentiments are shared by every actor and actress concerned in the enterprise – to help provide the Army Emergency Relief and the Navy Relief Society with the ways and means to carry on their valuable work."

Signed (James Cagney)

"Just to be invited was a great honor and we appreciate it." - Stan Laurel and Oliver Hardy. (Frame enlargement)

"Offering our time and effort to give what aid we can to the families of those in the fighting forces seems little enough to contribute to such a magnificent cause. I am pleased and honored that I have been asked to do my bit."

Signed (Rise Stevens)

Nothing matters these days except the winning of the war, and every one of us can help in some way or other -- no matter how unimportant our part may seem.

The Army and Navy Relief Fund and the Hollywood Victory Committee are doing great work. Personally, I'm getting a big thrill and a lot of fun out of doing my little bit with the Victory Caravan.

I hope the soldiers and sailors in our audiences are getting as much fun out of our efforts to entertain them as we are I meeting and greeting them. We've never played to such enthusiastic audiences in all our stage experience.

I want to thank the general public which is contributing so materially to the Army and Navy Relief Fund by attending our performances.

…. Charlotte Greenwood

I'm glad to say that every actor and actress in Hollywood is helping out with some sort of war work these days.

Every player I know who can spare a couple of weeks from picture-making hops out to the camps and does his or her little bit to cheer up the boys.

When the Hollywood Committee of the Army and Navy Relief Fund invited us to come along on their Victory Caravan it gave us all a big thrill. Just to be invited was a great honor and we appreciate it.

Audiences are showing us a big time, too. They make us feel that, after all, perhaps we actors can contribute a little something, too, toward making everybody happy in these times when national morale is so important.

….Laurel and Hardy

BIOGRAPHY OF BOB HOPE

Born in London, England, as one of a prolific family of seven brothers, Bob Hope came to this country in early youth. The family settled in Cleveland, where Bob received his schooling. After being graduated from high school, he went to work as a clerk for a motor company. He really started his career as an entertainer on that job…he was master of ceremonies at salesmen's meetings.

He has studied tap dancing and the yen for the footlights was strong in him. So after a while he worked up a dance act with a pal named George Byrne. They started in small time vaudeville opening at the Detroit State Theater, but they met with indifferent success both there and during subsequent engagements.

Remembering his debut as an amateur MC, Hope began to tell Scotch jokes and immediately audiences loved him. Thereafter he went solo. He toured the old Interstate Circuit and finally landed in New York, where his first appearance was at the Eighty-Sixth Street theater. After that the RKO circuit gave him a three-year contract as a headliner.

Vaudeville led to musical shows, notably "Ballyhoo", "Roberta", "Ziegfeld Follies" and "Red, Hot and Blue," then he went into radio.

Paramount signed him for "The Big Broadcast of 1938," in which he introduced the song hit "Thanks for the Memory," which has been his theme song ever since. His rise to a top spot on both the screen and the air has been phenomenal and he has just completed his fourteenth picture, "Road to Morocco" with Bing Crosby and Dorothy Lamour.

Cary Grant, the co-master of ceremonies is introduced by Bob Hope. (Frame enlargement)

RISE STEVENS

One year after Rise Stevens began formal training of her voice she was offered the greatest opportunity a young singer in America could hope for --- a contract with the Metropolitan Opera Company.

She turned it down!

In that decision lies her secret in success in the opera and concert fields – and the fact that motion pictures sought her.

A long-hoped for dream come true – and a hard decision to make, for Rise Stevens' dream of achieving the heights in grand opera goes back to her earliest childhood memory.

She rejected the offer because she didn't consider herself ready.

Born in New Your City on June 11, 1913, Miss Stevens is the second child of a typical average American family. Her father, Christian Steenberg, an advertising salesman, was born in Norway; her mother, Sarah, American born. A brother, Lewis, is following in his father's steps, selling advertising.

The high point of her grammar school years came when she was 10 years old. She made her first public appearance then, singing on the "Sunday Morning Children's Hour," produced by Milton Cross.

She attended New Town High School at Elmhurst, N.J. , and it was there she was introduced to light opera and the classics. She sang, she danced, she acted. Not a school play was presented that didn't find Rise Stevens among the cast. She was 17 when she first sang "The Chocolate Soldier."

Following graduation she was engaged for the Opera Comique series at the Heckscher Theater in Manhattan, where Madame Anna Schoen-Rene heard her and was impressed. A special scholarship at the Juilliard Graduate School of New York was obtained – and a great career was under way.

It was just a year later that Metropolitan Opera company executives heard her in audition at the Juilliard school. A contract was offered – and rejected. The rejection practically floored everyone connected with the Metropolitan.

In 1935 she went abroad for the first time, continuing her studies at the Mozartteum School at Salzburg, Austria. There she worked under the direction of Maria Gutheil-Schoder.

A week later she made her European debut at Prague, in the opera "Der Rosenkavalier," singing the role, Octavian and proved a great success in more ways than one.

Following her appearance there in her second role, that of Mignon, a strange man came backstage and presented her with a small stuffed rabbit. Wherever she appears today, that rabbit reposes on her dressing table. The man, Walter Szurovy, was playing at the same theater. He is now her husband.

Rise Stevens enjoys the applause after her numbers. (Frame enlargement)

She returned to New York in 1938, this time to accept the renewed offer of the Metropolitan. She made her American debut at Philadelphia in her favorite role of Octavian. The same week she was widely acclaimed by New York in her debut there as Mignon.

She left for England at the close of her first Metropolitan season, sang there that spring at the Mozart festival.

Early summer found her way to South America. She is the first American to have appeared at the famed Theatro Colon at Buenos Aires.

In 1940, her third season with the Metropolitan, she scored the most sensational success of her career to date as the temptress Delilah in "Samson and Delilah." Miss Stevens was the first American in 22 years to sing the fiery role with the Metropolitan.

It was also in 1940 that Miss Stevens traveled west to appear with the San Francisco Opera Company, where Metro-Goldwyn-Mayer first checked her as a possibility for pictures. A test was made – and a contract signed.

Miss Stevens adds to her theatrical abilities the love of walking, plays a good game of tennis, likes to swim.

###

UNIVERSAL STUDIOS   APRIL, 1942

CHARLES BOYER – BIOGRAPHY

LEGAL NAME:	CHARLES BOYER	HEIGHT:	5 FEET, 9 INCHES
BIRTHPLACE:	FIGEAC, FRANCE	WEIGHT:	150 POUNDS
BIRTHDATE:	AUGUST 28, 1899	COLORING:	BROWN HAIR
NATIONALITY:	FRENCH		BROWN EYES

If Figeac, France, never becomes noted for anything else, it will always be famous for producing one Charles Boyer. Little did the citizens of that hamlet know that when M. and Mne. Boyer announced the birth of Charles, that this same Charles would grow up, to be a screen lover par excellence, and to hold in his arms the world's crop of glamour girls sooner or later.

Boyer, who recently became a full-fledged citizen of the United States, which has been his home for more than 10 years, simultaneously assumed an even more portentous position than that implied by his popularity as a star. For in his future films effort he will function both as a star and as a producer under a new agreement with Universal Pictures.

M. Boyer, père, was a well-to-do dealer in farm machinery. Young Charles, active and restless, chaffed at the bit of parental control until they sent him to a parochial school. Here he astounded everyone by committing to memory the entire story of the Crucifixion while he was three years old. He was soon entered in the College Champollion, in Figeac, where, at age seven, he took part in a school celebration and recited so well that his efforts became a fixed part of such goings-on.

Amused at his son's dramatic abilities, the older Boyer turned over his granary to the boy for use as a theater, with Charles writing and acting in his own plays. Later, after the death of his father, Charles gave a series of benefit performances to aid Belgian refugees. He acted as stage manager, director and actor at these performances.

At the finish of his studies, he pursued his ambition, the stage, and soon was featured in the leading role of "L'Insoumise," a play written especially for him. It proved a sensation and Boyer became the idol of feminine hearts in Paris.

Hollywood sent for him to play leading roles in French versions of American pictures. He made "The Big House" and "The Trial of Mary Dugan." He set about learning the American language and in six months spoke it so well that he appeared with Ruth Chatterton and Ralph Bellamy in "The Magnificent Lie" for Paramount. He then alternated between French and English versions, and appeared with Jean Harlow in "The Red Headed Woman," and with Claudette Colbert in "The Man From Yesterday."

He met and married "Pat" Paterson, young English actress. The event broke an untold number of French and American hearts, it is reported. A trained musician, a fine athlete and one of the most talented stars of the screen, Boyer's is immensely popular in America. He is a crack tennis player, a good golfer, and adept at all winter sports.

Pictures include: "Love Affair," "All This and Heaven, Too," "Back Street," "Hold Back the Dawn," "Appointment For Love," "Tales of Manhattan," and "The Constant Nymph."

*****

Charles Boyer performing the "Last Class" dramatic vignette. A dark scene for a dark moment in history.

After declaring that France would be free again, he gave the Pledge of Allegiance. He had just become a citizen a short while before this tour. (Frame enlargements)

From Howard Strickling
Metro-Goldwyn-Mayer
Culver City, California

GROUCHO MARX

Groucho Is the mustached member of the Marxes.

His real name is Julius. He aquired the Groucho nickname as a youngster because his specialty was portraying crabby old men. Contrary to popular impression, he is not the oldest of the three Marx Brothers. He is the youngest.

Groucho was once a boy soprano in a Protestant Episcopal church and sang at a benefit for the San Francisco earthquake.

He is the most business-like of the Marxes.

He was indirectly responsible for Charlie Chaplin's entry into pictures. They met in Winnipeg, Canada, during vaudeville engagements, and Groucho urged Chaplin to accept $100 a week film job that had been offered him.

He claims that he still doesn't know what will make an audience laugh and what won't. Groucho says comedy is the biggest mystery in the world. Bigger than who killed Cock Robin.

Groucho has had the same leading lady, Margret Dumont, for the past ten years. His nickname for her is "Old Ironsides," because of the special corsets she wears to protect herself from sprains and strains in their tumultuous love scenes.

Groucho Marx in full make-up and cigar on stage. (Frame enlargement)

Max Eastman, in a magazine piece, wrote: "Groucho Marx without his make-up is a handsome and sensitive-featured young man with an exquisite profile, a man who might well, in a serious drama, play the part of Heinrich Heine."

He has written one book, one motion picture story, numerous magazine pieces.

Groucho likes to dress, off screen, in the height of correct fashion and looks like a leading man when not in make-up.

At fourteen, he was hired with two other boy singers as "The Leroy Trio." For a salary of $5 per week and expenses, they were to impersonate girls with their soprano voices.

The vaudeville tour lasted one week. At Denver, Groucho's voice changed overnight. He found himself stranded.

For weeks he drove a wagon between Victor and Cripple creek, Colorado, to get enough money for train fare back to New York.

Groucho's mustache is really a smear of greasepaint. He had worn crepe mustaches until he carelessly set fire to his mustache instead of his cigar one night.

He likes to swap costumes with Chico now and then, and play Chico's part during stage appearances.

The fact that he talks so fast he regards as an asset. Comments, "Take gag thieves. The only chance a gag thief would have would be if he learned stenography, and most of them haven't even learned English. There's no chance of a gag thief stealing anything during our tryout tours, especially if he hears it."

Groucho is married and has two children, Miriam and Arthur.

His favorite sport consists of going downstairs to play Mrs. Marx "for the ping pong championship of the world."

He's an excellent tennis player, and numbers Fred Perry among his close friends.

Groucho reads a great deal, and is the favorite comedian of the literati. He corresponds with Hugh Walpole, G. B. Stern, and Alexander Woollcott.

He likesikes to relax by playing on an ancient guitar, and will attempt anything, from "Home on the Range" to a Lohengrin Prelude or "The Bells of Kamenov."

His thirteen-year-old daughter, Miriam, made her stage debut during the San Francisco stop on a Marxian tryout tour. Harpo attired her in his spare wig and jockey costume, and sent her out on the stage to "crab" her "Old Man's" act. His nineteen-year-old son Arthur, is one of Southern California's outstanding tennis players.

He was born on October 21, 1890. He weighs 155 pounds, is five feet, seven and one half inches tall, has brown eyes, and black hair.

After "Room Service" at RKO, he returned to M-G-M for "At the Circus," "Go West" and "The Big Store." His first for M-G-M had been "A Night at the Opera, " and his second, was "Day at the Races." Previous pictures include "The Coconuts," "Animal Crackers," "Monkey Business," "Horsefeathers," and "Duck Soup."

###

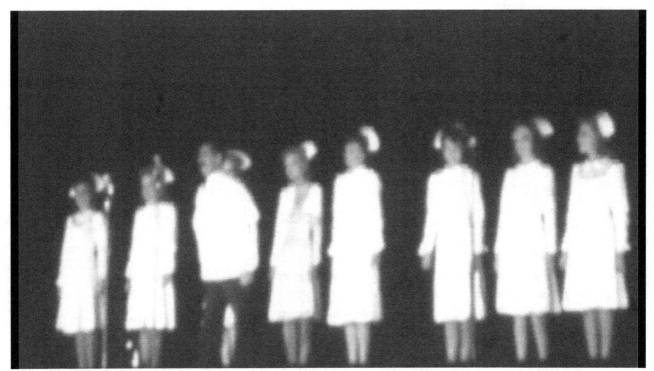

Groucho Marx in full make-up and cigar on stage.

Groucho sings "Dr. Hackenbush", a song not used in MGM's movie "A Day at the Races". (Frame enlargements)

BREIF BIOGRAPHY OF MERLE OBERON

Merle Oberon, christened Estelle Merle O'Brian Thompson was born on the Island of Tasmania on February 19, 1911. Her father, who died of pneumonia three months before the birth of his daughter, was an English army officer. Her mother was English and French-Dutch.

Until Merle was seven years old, she and her mother lived with a sister-in-law in Tasmania. She then accepted an invitation to stay with Lady Monteith, the child's godmother, in Bombay, India. The visit prolonged itself into a stay of two years. Then Mrs. Thompson went to join a brother in Calcutta.

During the next ten years in Calcutta, Merle was educated along the austere lines which her Army officer uncle deemed proper for one of his family. At 15 she became a member of the famous Calcutta Amateur Theatrical society and got a taste of the theater in her blood which settled the question of a career once and for all.

When Merle was not quite 17 her uncle got army leave for a trip to England and took the girl along. When it came time to return Merle begged to stay in Europe. She was determined to make a stage career for herself. The uncle let himself be persuaded and Merle remained behind to be watched over by family friends.

The first few months were extremely discouraging and finally in desperation Merle took a job as a dancer at the Café de Paris in London. Through this position she secured extra work in films and a year later was "discovered" by Alexander Korda and cast for a role in "The Wedding Rehearsal.'

Roles in one or two other films followed and then came the part of Anne Boleyn in "The Private Life of Henry Eighth." In this small role Merle achieved worldwide fame.

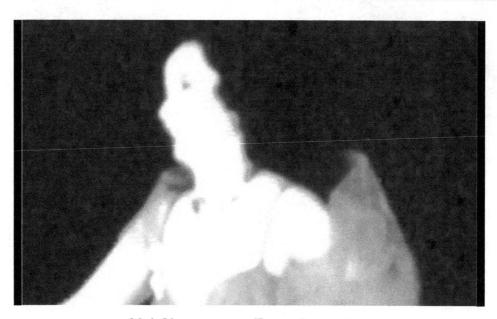

Merle Oberon, on stage. (Frame enlargement)

A short time later she came to Hollywood where she has appeared in a score of motion pictures including "The Dark Angel," "These Three," "The Scarlet Pimpernel," "The Cowboy and the Lady," "Wuthering Heights," "Till We Meet Again," "That Uncertain Feeling" and most recently the Alexander Korda production "Lydia."

Merle is five feet two inches tall, weighs 110 pounds, has chestnut hair, hazel eyes and tilted nose. Fond of clothes, she is exceedingly chic and considered one of the best dressed women in Hollywood. She loves jewels and has a splendid collection.

She is of a nervous temperament and quite superstitious, has a fondness for picking up pins and wishing on piebald horses. She is a good dramatic study and always knows her line; has a temper which she proudly boasts she has learned to curb; reads everything she can get her hands on, but prefers biographies. She likes animals and her favorite color is white. Her pet aversion is hats. She likes to change her hairdress frequently, also her makeup and perfumes.

She is the wife of Producer Korda, and they live in a big Georgian house in Bel Air in which they have gathered their painting and treasures.

PUBLICITY DEPARTMENT   April, 1942
COLUMBIA STUDIOS
HOLLYWOOD, CALIFORNIA

Biography

PAT O'BRIEN

The first time Pat O'Brien walked onto a stage he was a flop. He was nine years old and the Milwaukeeans who saw his first performance rumored around the town, "O'Brien's through."

It was a Christmas play at the parochial school of the Church of the Jesu in Milwaukee, where Pat was born November 11, 1899. He was cast as an angel with phony wings which he could flap by fluttering his elbows. He flapped them so hard that one fell off. When he stooped to pick it up, his nightshirt angel's robe ripped up the back.

That was in 1908, when O'Brien first abandoned the acting profession. He decided upon law and entered Marquette University. He was a better pitcher on the school's nine than a law student and was third stringer on the football team.

Somehow a false rumor was born that O'Brien made an immortal 95-yard run through the whole of Knute Rockne's Notre Dame team for the winning touchdown in the last minute of play. O'Brien denies it. Not only did it not happen, but he faced the South Bend Irish only once. They ran all over O'Brien and he limped back to the bench after the first few plays.

Again, in college, O'Brien returned to acting. He joined the dramatic club and debuted in a thing called "Foul Ball Kelly." Jimmie Gleason saw it and told O'Brien to drop in and see him should he ever go to New York.

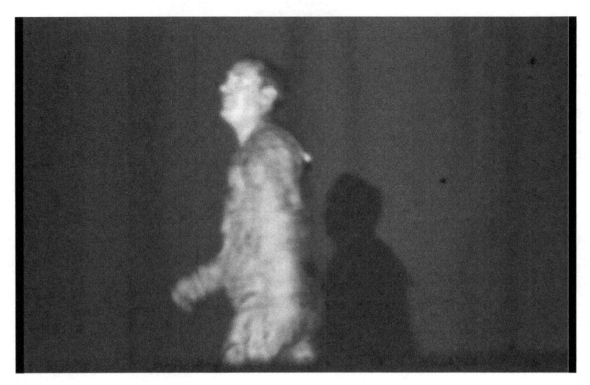

Pat O'Brien enjoys his standing ovation. (Frame enlargement)

Law practice did not appeal to O'Brien. Remembering Jimmie Gleason's invitation, he borrowed money from his parents, went to Sergeant School and renewed the Gleason friendship.

Gleason was producing a road company of "Way Down East," and gave O'Brien a job. A lean period rolled along – no work, no money, one meal a day and casting-office snubs.

O'Brien heard some chorus jobs were open in a musical, "Adrienne." He got one of the jobs and sang and danced. There wasn't much effeminacy in the show. Big, burly George Bancroft was the leading man.

Stock companies, road shows and very seldom Broadway jobs followed. O'Brien lived up in West 96th Street, off Broadway, at the time, in a $5-a-week room with Spencer Tracy.

On tour, O'Brien got acquainted with Frank McHugh in Des Moines. Frank introduced him to lovely Eloise Taylor, drafted as a kid from a dancing school to work in one of Frank's musicals.

Two years later, he again met Eloise in a road cast of "Broadway," delivering to her the greatest of all curtain lines, while playing Detective Dan McKern: "Pull yourself together, kid." He married her. The McHugh and O'Brien families have become a Hollywood legend of eternal friendship.

Soon after, "The Up and Up" became O'Brien's most advantageous play in New York and, through it, came his entrance into pictures.

Lewis Milestone, the director, dropped into the show one night. He had taken a party of movie people, including Marion Davies, to "The Green Pastures" at the Mansfield Theater across the street, but Milestone had seen the show twice before, so he left his guests to see "The Up and Up" for one act.

After "The Up and Up" closed, there was nothing in sight for O'Brien. It became tougher and tougher to pay $7 weekly rent and buy meals in one-arm restaurants.

One cold, wintery night he received a long distance telephone call from Hollywood. It was Howard Hughes, the young millionaire producer, on the wire. Hughes told O'Brien he badly needed a screwy reporter to play Hildy Johnson in "The Front Page." Lewis Milestone had recommended him. A few days later he was at work in Hollywood. Again, he was with his pal, Frank McHugh, who was playing the ukulele-strumming reporter who asks over the telephone, "Is it true, Madam, that you are the victim of a Peeping Tom?" Adolph Menjou was doing Burns, the managing editor and Everett Horton was the reportorial hypochondriac.

Right off, Hildy Johnson typed Patrick O'Brien, one of those Hollywood bugaboos. Part after part came along, but all the producers wanted of O'Brien was a fast-talking, snappily-moving, wisecracking, flashily-dressed young bozo.

A Warner contract was the next step, with O'Brien continuing as a fresh guy. Time again he worked with his pal McHugh and Jimmy Cagney, always losing the girl to Cagney, in such pictures as "Devil Dogs of the Air," and "The Irish In Us."

At last he had a chance to do something serious in "Oil For the Lamps of China." Other starring roles were in "Page Miss Glory," "Ceiling Zero," "Public Enemy's Wife," "Boy Meets Girl," "Angels With Dirty Faces," "Indianapolis Speedway," "The Kid From Kokomo," and the he topped all previous characterizations by playing Father Duffy in "The Fighting 69 th" and Rockne in "Knute Rockne."

Last year, O'Brien terminated his contract with Warner Brothers and moved over to Columbia to co-star with Constance Bennett in "Escape to Glory." He has been signed on long-term contract to Columbia and more recently has starred in "Two Yanks in Trinidad," with Brian Donlevy and Janet Blair, and in "He's My Old Man," with Glenn Ford and Evelyn Keyes.

With Mrs. O'Brien and their two children, Sean and Mavoureen, he lives at Brentwood, Calif., in a replica, on a smaller scale, of Mount Vernon.

* * * * *

From: Publicity Department
         RKO Radio Pictures, Inc
         Hollywood, California

BIOGRAPHY OF – CARY GRANT

Cary Grant was born in Bristol, England, on January 18, 1904. His real name is Archibald Leech. He ran away from school when he was 12 years old to join Bob Pender's acrobatic troupe which did eccentric dancing, stilt stunts and a clown routine. Four weeks later his irate father caught up with him and took him back to school.

His latent love for theatricals – undoubtedly inherited from his grandfather, Percival Leech, an English actor of renown – was fanned to fame when he conceived a new theatrical lighting effect. He took his idea to the manager of the Princess Theater in Bristol and was permitted to install and operate it for one show.

Association with show people led to his taking leave and joining up with Pender, and he but half-heartedly pursued his studies for another year and a half when he was brought back from that ill-starred expedition.

Later, he ran away from home again and rejoined Pender. Cary appeared as a "knockabout" comedian and at this time, knowing his heart was set on the profession, his father let him stay. When the troupe came to New York, young Grant came with it and appeared at the famous Hippodrome for two years.

Back in England, he spent two years with a stock company and developed an ability to sing. Arthur Hammerstein met him and signed him to a contract and brought him back in America in "Golden Dawn," and he has never returned to his native land since except for visits.

Many other musical comedy engagements followed, and during the summer of 1931 he appeared in twelve operettas as guess star if the St. Louis Repertoire company.

Then he appeared in "Nikki" with Fay Wray and Douglas Montgomery. After that Cary set out by automobile for Hollywood just on speculation. Luck evaded him and discouraged, he was about to head for Broadway again when he met a studio executive who arranged a screen test and two weeks later signed him to a long term contract.

"This is the Night" was his first picture. Since then he appeared in many productions. His first starring role was in "The Awful Truth" in which he shared honors with Irene Dunn.

Grant is unmarried and lives on his ranch near Saugus, driving into Hollywood daily, a distance of nearly 40 miles. He is six feet, one inch tall, weighs about 172 and has black hair and brown eyes.

His ranch is his hobby, and he raises horses and dogs as a profitable vocation.

Grant's most recent pictures include "Bringing Up Baby." "Holiday," "Gunga Din," "Only Angels Have Wings," "In Name Only," "His Girl Friday'" "My Favorite Wife," "The Howards of Virginia," "The Philadelphia Story, "Before the Fact," "Penny Serenade."

oOo

Cary Grant and Bert Lahr doing their Income Tax Sketch. Note the IRS workers sleeping in the background. The withholding tax on wages was introduced in 1943. Until then, people mailed their tax bills in. (Frame enlargement)

Claudette Colbert on stage. (Frame enlargement)

Biography of Claudette Colbert

Claudette Colbert arrived in Ney York City at the age of 13, from her native France. Her real name was Lily Chauchoin and her ambition was to be a dress designer.

A chance meeting with the friend of playwright, Ann Morrison, changed her mind and Mlle. Lilly pointed for the stage. When she landed her first three-line part in "The Wild Westcotts", she also changed her name.

Her first leading role was in a play which failed in Washington. But there were plenty of Broadway successes later, among them "The Ghost Train", "High Stakes", "Fast Life" and "The Barker".

She came to Hollywood in 1930, after signing a Paramount contract in the east, and has remained with that studio since. Her first picture was "Manslaughter". Majority of the 40 films to her credit were Paramount productions. The latest of them is "The Palm Beach Story", written and directed by Preston Sturges.

Miss Colbert was married to Dr. Joel Pressman, Hollywood physician, in Yuma, Arizona, in December, 1935. It was her second marriage. Her first husband was the actor, Norman Foster. Dr.

Pressman is now a Lieutenant, senior grade, in the Navy and is stationed in Pensacola.

The famous Colbert bangs are red-brown in color and she has brown eyes. Her figure is considered one of the most perfect on the screen. She is 5 feet. 4½ inches in height and she weighs 108 pounds.

* * *

From Howard Strickling

Metro-Goldwyn-Mayer Studios

Culver City, California

ELEANOR POWELL

Any particular sound that could become a dance at the drop of a heel and toe was for Eleanor Powell. On the other hand, she may conceive rhythm from a headline, or a day off at the beach. She recently got a tap dance from the telegraph, and danced a message in Morse Code.

Her talent is more than singular in the light of its origin. She first started dancing, almost driven to it by her mother, in order to overcome self-consciousness, it was never intended to become a profession.

She was born in Springfield, Massachusetts on November 21, 1912, the daughter of Clarence and Blanche Powell. Her father died in her infancy.

As a beginner at Ralph McKernan's dancing school, the girl suffered torture for a few weeks, then suddenly became his star pupil.

Eleanor Powell dancing for Victory. (Frame enlargement)

At thirteen, vacationing with her mother at Atlantic City, Eleanor was performing some childish routine on the beach on sand-piper legs with hair streaming in the wind. Gus Edwards happened to see her and at once persuaded Mrs. Powell to permit her to dance at the Ritz. The youngster became a seasonal attraction there until she was sixteen.

At first, New York wasn't receptive to Eleanor. Producers had conceded that she was an exceptional acrobatic dancer, but Broadway wanted rhythm. It was a tap town. Eleanor went to Jack Donahue for ten tap lessons, but still no part opened in a show until she got a tapping feature in "Follow Through."

It was the beginning of a rhythmic marathon that carried her through "Fine and Dandy," "Hot Cha," "Varieties," "Scandals," and "Crazy Quilt." She danced in "Casino de Paris" and became a name in lights.

In 1934 she received the title of "World's Greatest Tap Dancer" from the Dancing Masters of America.

With sound in the movies, Eleanor Powell was inevitably destined for Hollywood. She appeared at first on the screen in "George White's 1935 Scandals." Her next was Metro-Goldwyn-Mayer's "Broadway Melody of 1936." It started the whole country tapping. She was a star in her first picture.

Returning to Broadway for "At Home Abroad," she reappeared on the screen in "Born To Dance." In the interval, she has starred in a succession of musical pictures, with each more syncopating than its predecessor.

She lives with her mother in a home of English architecture in Beverly Hills.

Miss Powell is extremely popular. She never forgets a name, a face, or an anniversary. She is an expert swimmer and eats as she pleases.

* * *

<u>STATISTICS</u>

Born, Eleanor Powell, Springfield, Massachusetts on November 21, 1912. She was the daughter of Clarence and Blanche Powell; educated in public schools in Springfield; studied dancing with Ralph McKernan and Jack Donahue; Height, five feet, six inches; Weight, 123 pounds; Hair, chestnut; Eyes, blue; Occupations, dancer.

Stage plays: "Follow Thru," "Fine and Dandy," "Hot Cha," "Varieties," "Crazy Quilt," and "Casino de Paree" as a child at the Ritz in Springfield.

Pictures: "George White's Scandals," 1935; "Broadway Melody of 1936;" "Born to Dance," 1936; "Rosalie," Honolulu," 1937; "Broadway Melody of 1938;" "Broadway Melody of 1940;" "Lady Be Good," 1941; "Ship Ahoy," 1942.

From: Alexander Evelove
  Warner Bros. Studio
  Burbank, Calif. HO 6221

BIOGRAPHY

J O A N   B L O N D E L L

Born in New York City in 1909, Joan Blondell was reared in a property trunk for a while. Her father, Ed Blondell, was for twenty years a well-known comedian on the vaudeville stage, and his family not only traveled with him, but played in the act with him. By the time that Joan was able to walk out on stage, she also played a part.

Up to the time Joan was seven years old, each of her birthdays was celebrated in different countries. Then, until and including her twenty-second, each one was spent in a different city.

With all her traveling and acting, Joan took time, however, to get a thorough education. She attended high school in California and colleges in Denton, Texas, and New York City. She also clerked in a New York department store for the shortest time that anyone ever held a job – fifteen minutes – and ran a smart frock shop for the collegians in Denton.

It was soon after she had broken away from the family vaudeville troupe to appear in a stage production, "Penny Arcade," in New York City, that the movies discovered her. Warner Bros. bought the play and brought Joan and another young actor to the coast to play their original roles. That actor was James Cagney. The picture was released as "Sinner's Holiday."

Joan Blondell. (Frame enlargement)

Joan next scored as the breezy singer of Dorothy Mackaill in "Office Wife," and then played other comedy roles in close succession, in such pictures as "Illicit," "Other Man's Wife," "My Past," and "God's Gift to Woman." "Night Nurse," "Blonde Crazy," and "The Famous Ferguson Case" while still others gained added prestige from the blonde dynamo's presence.

It was not until Joan played the leading role in "Union Depot" opposite Douglas Fairbanks, Jr., however, that critics and public alike suddenly awakened to the fact that here was a sterling dramatic actress whose talents as a fast-talking comedienne were equaled by her emotional depth. "Miss Pinkerton" followed as her first starring picture, and "Three On a Match," and "Big City Blues" came next.

Joan was formerly married to George Barnes, one of Hollywood's most prominent cameramen. They had one child, Norman Scott Barnes. They were divorced in 1935 and Joan has since married Dick Powell, star of screen and radio and they have a daughter Susan. Powell has also legally adopted little Norman.

Her later pictures include "Footlight Parade'" "Goodbye Again," "Convention City," "We're In The Money," "Three Men On A Horse," "Gold-diggers of 1937," "The King and the Chorus Girl," "The Perfect Specimen," "I Want a Divorce," "Topper Returns," and "Model wife."

* * *

42342

From: Alex Evelove

Warner Bros. Studio
Burbank, Calif. HO 6221

BIOGRAPHY

JAMES CAGNEY

As soon as James Cagney was old enough to hold a job without the authorities interfering, he began to augment the family income by working after school and during summer vacations. The tow jobs he held first during his days as a student at Stuyvesant High School in New York City were those of office boy at the New York Sun and book page in a branch of the New York Public Library.

Meanwhile, it was his ambition to become an artist, because he displayed great talent at drawing and painting. The thought of becoming an actor never entered his mind.

Upon graduation from high school he entered Columbia University, but had to cut short the college education several months later when his father died. With his older brother, Harry, well advanced toward his goal of becoming a physician, Jimmy thought it incumbent on him to give up college and get a full-time job to help keep his family going. The family consisted of his mother, four boys and a baby girl.

Being unable to get such a job as he wanted – in the art department of a newspaper or advertising agency – he went to work in Wanamaker's department store, wrapping bundles for $12 a week. In the store he became friendly with a man who knew several fellows in a large vaudeville act. When one of the boys in the chorus of the act left it suddenly, Jimmy's friend suggested that he try to get the job.

The salary would be $25 a week, and that fact sold Jimmy on the idea. It was necessary for him to take some quick instruction in simple chorus dancing steps, and it was under this compulsion of necessity that Jimmy discovered he had a real talent for dancing.

He remained with the act three months, but left when a relative of his mother's obtained a job for him as a runner with a brokerage house. He held this job all of one summer, but his heart was elsewhere, for his three months in vaudeville had been sufficient to arouse in him an intense love for the theater. So, when the new season's show began to go into rehearsal early in the fall, Jimmy suddenly gave up his job and became a chorus man in the musical comedy, "Pitter Patter."

Meanwhile, he practiced his dancing assiduously when the show went on the road at the end of the season and all the other chorus boys were fired, he was retained in the capacity of specialty dancer.

At the end of that road tour, during which he married Frances Vernon, then a cute little chorus girl, he went back into vaudeville. During the next few years he worked in a great variety of vaudeville acts, most of them rather short-lived.

His first great opportunity came when, mainly because he was red-headed and aggressive-looking, he was given an audition for the leading role of the Maxwell Anderson play, Outside Looking In." He read that part so well that he was engaged to play it, he had the almost fairy-tale experience of making his Broadway debut in the leading role of what proved to be a successful play. And he won genuine acclaim from the critics for his portrayal of the part.

Jimmy Cagney performing "I'm a Yankee Doodle Dandy"   (Frame enlargement)

When the run of that play ended, he did not wait around for another Broadway engagement, he immediately went back into vaudeville. Soon, however, he was offered a role opposite Mary Boland in "Women Go On Forever," and when he took this part he deserted vaudeville forever.

The next season he staged the dances for "The Grand Street Follies, " and he both danced and acted in the production. This is what he did the following season, but between those two productions he also filled several stock engagements.

His next great step forward came when he received fulsome praise from the reviewers for his work in the George Kelly play, "Maggie the Magnificent." Another member of that cast whose acting drew favorable notice was Joan Blondell, and immediately after the close of the Kelly piece Jimmy and Joan were engaged for a play entitled "Penny Arcade."

Again both scored, and when Warner Bros. bought "Penny Arcade" to make into a picture which was subsequently given the title "Sinner's Holiday" both were brought to Hollywood to play in the screen version.

It was on April 16, 1930 that Jimmy arrived in Hollywood and before a year had elapsed he was one of the biggest stars in motion pictures. It was in his fourth picture, "Public Enemy," that he became an overnight sensation.

Since then he was consolidated his position by acting in a long list of pictures at Warner Bros., which has included "Smart Money," "Blonde Crazy," "Taxi," "The Crowd Roars<" "Winner Take All," "Hard to Handle," "Footlight Parade," "Lady Killer," "Here Comes the Navy," "A Midsummer's Night Dream," "G-men," "The Irish In Us," "Ceiling Zero," "Angels With Dirty Faces," "Each Dawn I Die," "The Roaring Twenties," "Fighting 69th," "Torrid Zone," "City for Conquest," "The Strawberry Blonde," "The Bride Came C.O.D.," "Captain of the Clouds" and "Yankee Doodle Dandy."

* * *   42342

From: Alex Evelove
      Warner Bros. Studio
      Burbank, Calif. HO 6221

BIOGRAPHY

OLIVIA de HAVILLAND

Olivia de Havilland's method of entrance into motion pictures made honest men out of all the fiction writers who have written the story of the little understudy stepping into a star's shoes on a moment's notice, saving the show and winning fame. Olivia went the fictionists one better. Her opportunity came when she became understudy to the understudy.

In the summer of 1934, Max Reinhart, noted impresario, was getting ready to stage "A Midsummer Night's Dream" at the Hollywood Bowl. Several months before the opening performance, an amateur presentation of the "Dream" was given by a group of community players headed by Dorothy Johnston at Saratoga, California, a hamlet of some 800 inhabitants. The dark-eyed Olivia, then 17, played the part of "Puck."

At this time the newspapers were full of Reinhardt's plans to present the Shakespearean play as a spectacle at the Bowl. Miss Johnston thought it would be an interesting experience for Olivia to sit in on the rehearsals conducted by the eminent producer, and with this thought in mind called on an old friend of hers, Catherine Sibley, assistant to Reinhardt.

Miss Sibley was entirely receptive to the idea and arranged a meeting between the fledgling actress and Felix Weissberger, who was casting the show. Weissberger, to everyone's amazement, asked Olivia to read a few lines of the "Dream" and then told her she might not only attend rehearsals but she might also understudy.

The part of "Hermia" was set for Gloria Stuart. Jean Rouverol understudied the role and Olivia understudied Jean. Within a few days after rehearsals began, however, Jean was called to Paramount for a picture with W. C. Fields, and since Gloria was herself busy on a film at Warner Bros., Olivia rehearsed as Hermia for the following three weeks.

Suddenly, six days before the premiere of the "Dream," the news came through that Gloria's picture schedule was to run longer than had been expected and a substitute would have to be found. Olivia was prepared. Olivia's triumph in the glamorous spectacle was immediate and lasting. When it closed at the Bowl, Reinhardt took it on the road and she went along. There was no one else but Olivia who would do for the role of Hermia when Reinhadrt filmed "A Midsummer Night's Dream" as a Warner Bros. Picture.

Placed under long term contract by Warner Brothers, Olivia was at once cast in a couple of pictures so she could acquire film experience. First of these was "Alibi Ike," staring Joe E. Brown, in which she was the leading lady. Then she had the leading feminine role in "The Irish In Us" with Jimmy Cagney, Pat O'Brien and Frank McHugh.

About that time an unknown by the name of Errol Flynn appeared on the scene. Studio officials had so much faith in his talent and potential box office power that they decided to star him in "Captain Blood," a gigantic spectacle-romance. They knew it was a gamble, so they decided to double the gamble by taking a chance on another comparative unknown, casting Olivia opposite Flynn.

The gamble proved a sure-thing bet. Olivia and Flynn were sensations and the picture was a huge box office success. Another record breaker followed in "The Charge of the Light Brigade."

Next Olivia starred in "Call It A Day," with Ian Hunter as her leading man. Then she filmed "It's Love I'm After," with Leslie Howard; "The Great Garrick," "Gold Is Where You Find It," The Adventures of Robin Hood," "Four's a Crowd," "Hard To Get," "Wings of the Navy," and played the important part of Melanie in "Gone With the Wind" for Selznick-International Studio. Returning to her home lot, she made "My Love Came Back," "Santa Fe Trail," went over to Paramount to make "Hold Back The Dawn," and was back at Warner Brothers again appearing in "The Strawberry Blonde," "They Died With Their Boots On," "The Male Animal" and "In This Our Life."

Born in Tokyo, Japan, of British parents, Olivia was brought to this country when she was two years old, and she legally became an American citizen several months ago. She has resided in Hawaii, San Francisco and Saratoga, California. She was educated at Saratoga Grammar School, Notre Dame Convent, and Los Gatos High School and had won a scholarship to Mills College, Berkeley, when opportunity beckoned her to "A Midsummer Night's Dream."

* * *

42342

Olivia de Havilland performing "Who's Olive?" with Groucho Marx. (Frame enlargement)

BIOGRAPHY OF MARK SANDRICH

Mark Sandrich, producer-director of the Hollywood Victory Caravan, has long been famed in the motion picture world as one of the ace directors of genuine entertainment. More than any other creator in pictures, he has devoted his talents to the successful presentation of singing, dancing and music on the screen, legitimately incorporated in a motion picture story.

Beginning with Fred Astaire - Ginger Rogers pictures for RKO-Radio some eight years ago, such as "The Gay Divorcee," "Top Hat," "Follow The Fleet," "Shall We Dance" and "Carefree", Sandrich has developed this form of entertainment to the highest degree. Most recently he produced and directed the Jack Benny pictures at Paramount, "Man About Town", "Buck Benny Rides Again" and "Love Thy Neighbor", the latter co-starring Fred Allen.

He deviated from his musicals long enough to make one of the best legitimate comedies of last year, "Skylark", staring Claudette Colbert with Ray Milland and Brian Aherne.

His most recent production for Paramount is said to be his best. It is "Holiday Inn", co-starring Bing Crosby and Fred Astaire to Irving Berlin's music. This picture, which has a Berlin hit song for every great American holiday, will be Paramount's special attraction for the fall season, released on Labor Day.

Born in New York City, educated at Columbia University, - but like most ace picture directors Mark Sandrich came up the ladder the hard way, learning his "trade" as a gag man, film cutter, cameraman, writer, assistant director and finally director of two reel comedies.   424-23

From: Publicity Department
  RKO Radio Pictures, Inc.
  Hollywood, California

BIOGRAPHY OF - DESI ARNAZ

Desi Arnaz (pronounced Dessy Ar-naz) was born at Santiago, Cuba, on March 2, 1917. It's his real name and also that of his grandfather who fought on the American side at the battle of San Juan Hill during the Spanish-American war. He is five feet ten and one-half inches tall, weighs 160 pounds. His hair is black and his eyes are such a dark brown they appear black. He was educated at Colegio de Dolores, Jesuit prep school, at Santiago, Cuba and at St. Patrick's High School, Miami Beach, Florida.

Desi's boyhood was happy. His father, then mayor of Santiago, was wealthy and Desi had everything a boy's heart could desire. In 1933 the Cuban revolution broke out, Arnaz, Sr., was thrown in prison with the other congressmen and his wealth and land were confiscated. Six months later when he was released the impoverished man fled to Florida with his wife and son. He since has returned to Cuba and is active in politics.

Desi Arnaz performing his "Cuban Pete" number. (Frame enlargement)

Completion of Desi's high school education continued hit and miss fashion over several years because of low family finances. He worked awhile, went to school until the money ran out, worked again. His early ambition was to become a criminal lawyer.

One of those early jobs was cleaning bird cages and restocking them with food for a man who rented canaries to most of the drug stores in Miami Beach. He was paid $15 per week for this. He also worked with his father who had started a small importing business, specializing in roof tiles and other pottery importations.

When Desi was seventeen he started singing with a band at the Roney-Plaza Hotel at Miami Beach. He remained there two seasons, then appeared at the same hotel with his own seven-piece rumba band. Xavier Cugat saw him at a tea dance at the Roney-Plaza and signed him to sing with his band. Desi joined Cugat's band in July 1939, remained with it as a singer until December of that year. Then Desi went to La Conga at Miami with his own band and was such a sensation that Cugat wanted to sign him to a ten-year contract.

After this successful season Desi returned to Cuba but found no opportunity there. Rather than accept an office position, he borrowed $150 and returned to New York, arriving there with $60. He was unable to find a job for four months. Then he was hired to put a band into Fran and Bill's, a popular nightclub at Glenn Falls, near Saratoga, N.Y. as the featured attraction. Remaining there from July to Labor Day, he returned to New York and played a two-week engagement at the Central Park Casino.

Out of a job again in November, he went to Miami where he again took his own band into La Conga. Before long his band became the main attraction at La Conga.

Though he has played in school dramatics at Colegio de Doloris in Cube and had sung in school musicals at St. Patrick's High School in Florida, he had never entertained an ambition to go to the stage. His opportunity to go on the stage came in a strange way.

George Abbott was planning production of "Too Many Girls" but was experiencing difficulty in finding anybody to play the part of Manuelito, the South American football flash. Abbott was an expert dancer and danced frequently to the music of Desi's rumba band at La Conga in New York.

Lorenz Hart, who, with Richard Rodgers, wrote the musical numbers for "Too Many Girls," also knew the music and work of Desi Arnaz. It occurred simultaneously to Abbott and Hart that Desi was the ideal choice to play Manuelito. He accepted the assignment and was an immediate hit. The show opened in October 1939 and ran until shortly before production started on its picturization.

Desi sings baritone on the tenor side, dances, plays the guitar and conga drums. He introduced the Conga dance in Miami, and the Conga line in New York. In the latter city he also introduced the custom of dancers carrying farolas, or lamps, as native Cuban dancers do.

In school he played basketball and soccer. He was a member of the Colegio de Dolores varsity soccer team which won the Cuban championship one year. In New York he kept fit through daily workouts in a gymnasium. He swims, plays tennis and handball and bowls. Football, good boxing matches, and baseball are his favorite spectator sports. His favorite dish is chicken and rice, a native Cuban dish, and his pet aversion is being awakened by early morning telephone calls.

Arnaz was brought to Hollywood in June 1940, to play his original role in "Too Many Girls" in the screen version of the stage show filmed by RKO Radio Pictures. It was in this picture that he met Lucille Ball, who later became his wife. Following the completion of the film, Arnaz went out on a personal appearance tour and Miss Ball went East to join him. They were married in Greenwich, Conn. on Nov. 30, 1940.

In the spring of 1941, Desi and his bride returned to Hollywood and he went into RKO Radio's "Father Takes a Wife." The Arnaz home is in Northridge, in the San Fernando Valley.

oOo

Desi Arnaz shows off his Conga rhythm. (Frame enlargement)

From: Alex Evelove
      Warner Bros. Studio
      Burbank, Calif. HO 6221

BIOGRAPHY

F R A N K   McH U G H

Frank McHugh has been around since he embarked in the theatrical business with his parents, playing a child role, in "For Her Children's Sake." That was in 1909 in New England, ten years after his birth in Homestead, Pa., May 23,1899.

He is one of the four children of Edward A. and Catherine McHugh. He attended St. Peter's grammar school in Pittsburgh and completed his education between theatrical engagements.

"For Her Children's Sake" and "Human Hearts," which followed it, played one night stands throughout the New England states and was pretty much a family affair, with the mother, father, sister and two brothers enacting the principle roles.

Later, in Pittsburg, Frank played child roles with the Harry Davis Stock Co. and for two years he toured with small companies in that same district.

At seventeen, he graduated from child roles and became a juvenile. He also became a stage manager for the Marguerite Bryant players at the Empire theater in Pittsburgh. A year later Frank joined the Sherman Kelly Stock Company and toured the Middle West in repertoire. Then he went into vaudeville and toured the Orpheum and Keith circuits for two years. Joining resident stock companies at Waterbury and Bridgeport, Connecticut, he remained in New England three years before moving West to work in other resident stock companies.

Frank played stock in Baltimore with Spencer Tracy and went to London as understudy for the "Is Zat So" company with James Gleason. He made his Broadway bow in 1925 with Gleason in "The Fall Guy." After that he did the part of a cockney in "Fog" and followed that with "Tenth Avenue" in which Frank Morgan was starred. His best Broadway role was in "Excess Baggage" with Miriam Hopkins. The same year he made his screen bow in a talking short entitled, "If Men Played Cards As Women Do."

He went to Hollywood in January, 1930, and gave outstanding comedy performances in "Top Speed," "The Dawn Patrol," "The Front Page," and other films. His splendid work in "One Way Passage" with William Powell and Kay Francis won him a Warner Bros. Contract, under which he remained at that studio a number of years.

In June, 1933, he married the former Miss Dorothy Spencer of Hartford, Conn. They have three children, Peter, Susan and Michael.

Among the outstanding pictures in which he has appeared are: "Blessed Event," "Elmer the Great," "Lily Turner," "Footlight Parade," "Convention City," "Here Comes the Navy," "Devil Dogs of the Air," "A Midsummer Night's Dream," "The Irish in Us," "Three Men on a Horse," "Submarine D-1," "Boy Meets Girl," "Four Daughters," "Wings of the Navy," "Daughters Courageous," "Dodge City," "Dust Be My Destiny," "The Roaring Twenties," "Four Wives" and "The Fighting 69th."

***   42342

National Broadcasting Company

Sunset and Vine,   Hollywood

April 23, 1942
          Biography:

FRANCES LANGFORD

Singing Star of Bob Hope's NBC Program

A pair of yanked tonsils changed Francis Langford's entire life! A tonsillectomy turned her clear soprano voice into the deep rich contralto which has won her fans and fortune because of its unusual quality.

When Miss Langford was a soprano, singing in church choirs in her hometown, Lakeland, Florida, her first ambition was to become an opera singer. Born on April 4, 1913, she attended grammar and high school at Lakeland, and later went to Southern College where she majored in music.

Upon graduation from college she found herself minus tonsils and her grand opera singing voice; her house of cards tumbled! But her mother, a concert pianist, encouraged her to train the strange deep voice that had come as a result of the operation, and assured her heartbroken daughter that she would win fame in another field.

And fame it was for the little elfin-faced singer. She was a hit on her first radio broadcast as a "blues" singer and her popularity in Florida redoubled as a result of her new voice. National fame came when Rudy Vallee, who was making a personal appearance in Florida, signed her to appear on his New York radio program.

Following her appearance on the Vallee program, she was signed for the musical show, "There Goes the Bride". It proved to be a jinxed show, which folded shortly after it opened. Following this venture she formed her own vaudeville act and toured the country with great success. NBC nabbed her when she returned to New York. Her new contract permitted her to sing in night clubs and hotels and make personal appearance tours. She was given featured spots in three national radio programs, which resulted in one of the largest batches of fan mail ever received by any air star.

Walter Wanger was the key to her entrance into pictures. While in New York searching for fresh movie talent, he heard Miss Langford sing at a party given at the Waldorf-Astoria Hotel for Cole Porter. The producer asked the attractive singer how she would like to give Hollywood a tryout.

In private life she is Mrs. Jon Hall and spends her leisure hours swimming, horseback riding, and playing tennis. She is also a camera fiend and many of her Sundays are spent clicking unusual film shots.

She is a great reader of historical novels and plays. Her favorite playwright is Eugene O'Neill..

Although she has won her fame as a swing exponent in music, her tastes run to the classics and Tchaikovsky is her favorite composer.

Five feet three, Miss Langford weighs a little over a hundred pounds, and her brown hair matches her large brown eyes.   ---

Frances Langford sings. (Frame enlargement)

Short Biography of <u>Jerry Colonna</u>

Born in Boston, 38 years ago, christened Gerard Colona, Jerry's first memories are those of being taken by his mother to the Boston Opera House to hear the famous tenor, Enrico Caruso. Although brought up in an atmosphere of art and culture, Jerry favored hanging out by the corner grocery store, rolling his eyes and striking characteristic poses of opera stars.

At the age of 14, he had his own orchestra and played at socials, weddings and political rallies. He was once labeled Boston's first jazz skin beater. After he mastered the trombone, Leo Reisman took him away from "smalltime stuff". Six months later, Ozzie Nelson doubled his salary, taking him away from Reisman. Soon, he became well-known as a singing comedian and Fred Allen put him on the air as a guest artist.

Hollywood spotted him not long after, while he was a member of Peter Van Steeden's band.

He appeared in the musicals, "Fifty-Second Street" and "Rosalie". Starting to make records for Brunswick, his first, "Hector the Garbage Man", sold more than 100,000 platters. Bing Crosby made him guest artist on his radio program. Bob Hope heard him, recognized the kind of talent he was looking for, and signed Colonna for his own radio show.

During the time he was making "Road To Singapore", in which he was featured with stars Crosby, Hope, and Dorothy Lamour, he was voted "Oomph Man Number 1 of Hollywood" by Madeleine Carroll, Paulette Goddard, Lana Turner and Ann Sheridan.

Married to Florence Purcell, Colonna is 5 feet 10 inches tall, weighing 160 pounds. His now-famous moustache is 12 inches long from end to end. Yes, it's real.

He is featured in Paramount's "True To The Army" with Ann Miller and Judy Canova. He stars in "Priorities of 1942", an aircraft musical, again with Ann Miller and with Vera Vague, Betty Rhodes and Johnny Johnston. In this film, he returns to his trombone playing and to a rough-cut band.

* * *

Jerry Colonna and Bob Hope before Colonna's trumpet solo. (Frame enlargement)

BIOGRAPHY

of

JOAN BENNETT

Among the few royal families of actors whose ancestry in the thespian line dates back to other centuries the Bennetts have perhaps the tallest family tree. It goes back further than the Barrymores and the Tyrone Powers and the Lupinos.

The youngest of this clan is Joan Bennett whose ancestors were Scotch and English strolling minstrels and players of centuries ago. Her maternal ancestors were the famous Wood family of actors in England. Her great grandfather, William Wood, married Sarah Campbell, direct descendant of the Duke of Argyle, so there is also royal blood in Joan 's veins. William Wood, after playing in England, came to America with five sons and Joan's grandmother.

All the children went on the stage in America -- her great uncle, Alfred, was a musician, the rest of the boys and her grandmother, Rose Wood, danced.   The latter made her debut at the age of eight in the entre-acts of the big plays. Rose Wood later became a great New York star and played with the Drews, Barrymores and Joseph Jefferson.

Rose's cousins, Rosina and Theresa Vokes, English actresses became well known in America. Her grandfather was Lewis Morrison, a star in his own right for over thirty years and who co-starred with James O'Neill, Forest Salvina, Edwin Booth and Barrett.

The youngest daughter of Richard Bennett, famous stage and screen star, and Adrienne Morrison was born in Palisades, New Jersey, on February 27, 1910. Joan two older sisters, Constance and Barbara, were considered the beauties of the family who were destined to carry on the family acting tradition. Little Joan was considered too mousey a person to be a family torchbearer.

Until she was eight years old, Joan was tutored privately in New York and was then sent to St. Margaret's boarding school in Waterbury, Conn. Later she was sent to a finishing school L'Ermitage, at Versailles, France, and to a private school in London.

Joan was not a pretty child. Constance, blonde and stately, and the brunette Barbara, were considered the beauties. Joan's hair was of indefinite shade and was always combed back plainly with a huge bow perched on top of her head. She developed near-sightedness and had to wear glasses. No one paid any attention to this ugly little duckling, and as a result she became shy and developed an inferiority complex.

It was this complex, Joan admits, that led her to run away from school in England and elope in 1926 - when she was sixteen years old, with John Marion Fox of Seattle, Wash. Joan just wanted to show her sisters that though she was not as gorgeous as they, she could at least win a husband.

Joan Bennett "dismantling an automobile." (Frame enlargement)

Her husband was a young student in London, and two years after their marriage, they returned to America where her first daughter, Diana Bennett Fox, was born on February 20, 1928. The marriage was dissolved by divorce late in 1928.

All of Joan's schooling had specialized in languages, music and interior decorating. She had no intention or desire to follow an acting career. Several acting offers came the way of the daughter of the famous Richard Bennett, but she was definitely not interested.

She wanted to open an interior decorating shop in New York and she tried to induce her mother to give up her stage career and go into business with her. The shop never did materialize.

It was only because she was badly in need of money that she accepted her father's offer for a role in "Jernigan." Without any stage experience at all, she took the part which kept her on the stage all the way through the first act and part of the second.

This success brought her an offer of the lead in "Hotbed," a Brook Pemberton production. Although the salary was four times what she had gotten before, she took her father's advice to turn it down. The play proved a failure, and Joan was thankful for her father's counsel.

Hollywood had already noticed her, and although she had never thought of the movies as a career, even while acting on the stage, she accepted the flattering offer to play with Ronald Colman in "Bulldog Drummond." following this, she was signed to a contract by the Art Cinema Corporation, United Artists producers. Under this, her first role was the feminine lead in "Three Live Ghosts." Next came "Disraeli" in which she supported George Arliss. Then she shared honors with Joseph Schildkraut in "The Mississippi Gambler." She attracted a great deal of attention when she played opposite Harry Richman in "Puttin' On The Ritz," which led to her being secured by Fox for "Crazy That Way." She followed this with the lead opposite John Barrymore in "Moby Dick," and then a long string of pictures followed in rapid succession.

Joan Bennett was established as a screen star in a career that was to go on year after year for many years. Even when her sister Barbara retired from acting, and Constance made infrequent pictures, Joan, who was once thought to be too mousey for an acting career, became the standard bearer of the acting Bennetts.

On March 16, 1932, she married Markey, producer and writer, by whom she had another daughter, Melinda, born on February 27, 1934, Joan's own birth date. She was divorced from Gene Markey in June, 1937.

Her third and present marriage was to the producer Walter Wanger, which took place in Phoenix, Arizona.

Only once did Joan Bennett interrupt her screen career to accept a stage role. In the fall and winter of 1937 she traveled throughout the East in the road production of "Stage Door" in the star role of Terry Randall.

She was a big success in this role, and brought back memories of her childhood when, although she was not considered an actress, she directed her sisters in plays. When she was eight years old, she staged and directed a playlet called "Timid Agnes and the Mouse," featuring Constance and Barbara. She charged her father, mother, and friends one dollar admission to this home production. The venture was a success and encouraged her to repeat it with other playlets. She was always the director and never the actress, but her sisters took her direction willingly.

Realizing what her early childhood was like, Joan does everything in her power to bring her two daughters up to have confidence in themselves and to train them to be beautiful, believing it to be one of woman's greatest assets.

She does the interior decorating of her own home and is known as one of Hollywood's outstanding hostesses.

The most exciting time she had in her life was when, at the age of 15, she spent an April in Paris.

Like most theatrical folk, she is quite superstitious. Will not light three on a match, knocks on wood, won't walk under ladders, is afraid of black cats and the number "13" and is a salt-over-the-shoulder thrower. Won't permit love birds, goldfish or ivy in the house because they are bad luck. Elephant statuettes must have trunks up, and she believes that if you sing before breakfast, you cry before supper.

Her favorite color is turquoise blue, her favorite flowers are Lady Finch roses and gardenias, her favorite perfume is Gardenia, and the book she remembers most pleasantly is "Beverly of Graustark."

Her most memorable moment in Hollywood was the day in 1929 when she was rushed from the train where the late director Dick Jones introduced her to Ronald Colman and told her she would play opposite him in "Bulldog Drummond."

She says the most helpful stars she ever worked with were Claudette Colbert and Warner Baxter.

Her children and her home are her main hobbies. Next in importance is her hobby of collecting rose quartz.

She is considered one of Hollywood's smartest dressed woman. Her hair is naturally golden blonde, which she changed not long ago to black - just to be different. Her eyes are blue and she stands five feet, three inches in height and weighs 110 pounds.

VITAL STATISTICS

REAL NAME:	Joan Bennett
BIRTHPLACE:	Palisades, New Jersey
BIRTHDATE:	February 27, 1910
HEIGHT:	5 feet - 3 inches
WEIGHT:	110 pounds
HAIR:	Golden blonde
EYES:	Blue

MARRIED TO: John Marion Fox in 1926, divorced in 1928; Gene Markey in March 16. 1928, divorced in 1937; Walter Wanger in Phoenix, Ariz., January 13, 1940.

CHILDREN: Diana Bennett Fox, born on February 20, 1928.
Melinda Morrison Bennett, born on February 27, 1934.

MOTHER: Adrienne Morrison Bennett (deceased)
FATHER: Richard Bennett

EDUCATION: St. Margaret's Boarding School, Waterbury Connecticut; L'Ermitage, Versailles, France.

oOo

BIOGRAPHY OF JOAN BENNETT

PICTURE RECORD:

1928
BULLDOG DRUMMOND - UA
THREE LIVE GHOSTS   - UA

1929
DISRAELI - Warners
THE MISSISSIPPI GAMBLER - Univ.

1930
PUTTIN" ON THE RITZ - UA
CRAZY THAT WAY - Fox
MOBY DICK - Warners
MAYBE IT'S LOVE - Warners
TWO IN A CROWD - Univ.

1932
CARELESS LADY - Fox
SHE WANTED A MILIONAIRE - Fox
WEEENDS ONLY - Fox
I MET MY LOVE AGAIN - UA
ME AND MY GAL - Fox
THE TRIAL OF VIVIENNE WARE
 -Fox
WILD GIRL - Fox

1933
LITTLE WOMEN - RKO

1934
THE PURSUIT OF HAPPINESS - Para.
THE MAN WHO RECLAIMED HIS
HEAD   - Univ.

1935
MISSISSIPPI - Para.
PRIVATE WORLDS - Para.
TWO FOR TONIGHT - Para
SHE COULDN'T TAKE IT - Col.
THE MAN WHO BROKE THE
BANK AT MONTE CARLO - TCF

1936
13 HOURS BY AIR - Para.
BIG BROWN EYES - Para
WEDDING PRESENT - Para.
TWO IN A CROWD - Univ.
WEDDING PRESENT - Para.

1937
VOGUES OF 1938 - UA

1938
I MET MY LOVE AGAIN - UA
TRADE WINDS - UA - Wanger
THE TEXANS - Para.
ARTIST AND MODELS ABROAD
- UA

1939
THE MAN IN THE IRON MASK
- UA
THE HOUSEKEEPER'S
DAUGHTER -UA   -Roach
 ARIZONA TO BROADWAY -Fox
GREEN HELL - Univ.

1940
HOUSE ACROSS THE BAY - UA
THE SON OF MONTE CRISTO
- UA

1941
MAN HUNT - TCF
WILD GEESE CALLING - TCF
CONFIRM OR DENY - TCF
TWIN BEDS - UA - Small

1942
HIGHLY IRREGULAR - Col.

A. M. BOTSFORD
PUBLICITY DIRECTOR
20th CENTURY-FOX
HOLLYWOOD

BIOGRAPHY

OF

<u>LAUREL AND HARDY</u>

Having appeared together in 169 pictures during the past 17 years, Stan Laurel and Oliver Hardy are almost as much a part of each other as Siamese twins -- both in the eyes of the public and of themselves.

They have dropped the pronoun "I" from their conversations and even when discussing some of the few matters which affect only one of them, they use the royal plural. Perhaps this is one of the reasons that they are able to say that in all of their long association they have never had so much as one cross word - a record absolutely without parallel in the history of comedy teams.

It is worth explaining here that the one time the boys did separate was due to contractual difficulties with their former producer and not to any dispute with each other. Stan had been under contract for some months when Ollie was signed and so each year the producer only had to deal with one of them at a time and Laurel and Hardy were never able to put up a united front in negotiations.

This situation prevailed for years and finally in 1939, Stan refused to talk contract until Ollie's deal had expired. The producer then teamed Hardy with Harry Langdon in a picture called "Zenobia." The experiment was not repeated and the boys were brought back together again.

In the Spring of 1941, 20th Century-Fox was looking for comedians so that the studio might participate in the great vogue for slapstick comedy, a result, probably, of war psychology. Laurel and Hardy were caught on a personal appearance tour, without film contractual obligations, and on June 6, were signed to make two pictures a year for the next five years. Their first vehicle was a draft comedy entitled "Great Guns," produced by Sol M. Wurtzel.

Laurel and Hardy are the great comedy team of motion pictures! Now and again, a team like Wheeler and Woolsey or Abbott and Costello will flash into huge success in films, but none of them have ever approached the great worldwide success of Stan and Ollie. Not in continuous years of popularity nor in the geographical scope of it.

The formation of this record breaking entertainment combination was completely accidental and rather remarkable since the two men came from contrasting background and after each had made quite a name by himself.

Stanley Laurel was born in Ulberstone Lancs., England, on June 16, 1890, to Arthur Jefferson Laurel, comedian and producer, and Madge Metcalfe, a dramatic actress of considerable repute. Stan was "raised in a trunk" in the time honored tradition of the offspring of show people and made his first stage appearance at the age of seven in a drama called "Lights of London." For the next few years he varied the monotony of life at King James public school and Queen's Park School, in Glasgow, with occasional work in the theater. Finally, at the age of 15, he left school for good and joined a variety troupe as a song and dance man.

In 1910, Stan came to the United States as an understudy to Charles Chaplin in a troupe called "The London Comedians" whose impresario was Fred Karno. This group toured America from one end to the other and finally broke up when Chaplin joined Mack Sennett. Stan went on in vaudeville on his own hook until 1917, when he came to Universal as a comedian. For one reason or another, this venture didn't quite come off and he returned to the stage for five more years.

Again Stan returned to Hollywood, but this time as a writer and director. He was directing a picture staring Theda Bara in which Oliver Hardy was to have played a butler. Hardy suffered a bad burn on his arm in an accident on the set and when no one else could be found to play the part, Stan stepped in and did it himself.

He did it so well, as a matter of fact, that he kept acting, despite his strenuous objections. About a year later, in 1924, he and Hardy were cast in the same picture. One called "Home from the Honeymoon." The boys say they liked each other from the very first, but that the idea of teaming for comedy didn't seriously occur to them until they had done five ot six pictures together and were in fact already a comedy team.

Stan is married to Mrs. Virginia Ruth Laurel and has a 13-year-old daughter, Lois, by a previous marriage. They live in San Fernando Valley on an interesting acre of ground surrounded by a six foot brick wall with the name "Fort Laurel" over its massive gate. The place was formerly a chicken ranch which Stan, by laying 200,000 bricks and planting innumerable plants, has transformed into a wonderfully comfortable and attractive home. Stan's chief recreation these days is working in his garden and he has been experimenting in hybrids with results more amusing than practical.

Oliver Hardy was born on January 18, 1892, in Harlem, Ga., to Oliver Hardy Sr. (deceased) lawyer and hotel keeper, and Mrs. Emily Hardy. He attended public schools in Harlem and in Atlanta and also Georgia Military Academy, where he also played guard on the football team. However, the glee club was the activity that really interested him - - he has a fine tenor voice - - and at the end of his sophomore year he departed from school to join a minstrel show.

Three years passed and his troupe was in Jacksonville, Fla., where the old Lubin Film Co., had its studio. The company wanted a fat comedian. Ollie was about the same build that he is now and so they got together. That same year - - it was 1915 - -the company came to Hollywood and brought Hardy with them. Hardy was a featured comedian from that time until he and Stan achieved stardom together.

Ollie and his wife, Mrs. Lucille Jones Hardy, also live in the San Fernando Valley, about eight miles from Stan. Hardy used to be a golf fiend and shot a very good game, indeed, being on a par with Bing Crosby and other famous fellow members of Lakeside Golf Club. In the last couple of years Ollie has returned to the soil, however, and like Stan spends a great deal of time gardening. He, also, has an acre which was formerly devoted to the raising of chickens. In fact, he and Stan have converted an incubator into a theater where they have a fine stage, motion picture projectors and all the trappings of a full scale film house. The Hardy home features unpretentious comfort, but does boast a swimming pool. The Hardy's have no children. They have a chow dog named Toy.

The comedy of Laurel and Hardy is essentially pantomime which is in part responsible for their tremendous European success though the boys have had enough dialogue in the foreign versions of their pictures so that they have acquired a speaking knowledge of five different languages. As they worked together they gradually developed their distinct style. They were the first comedians to slow the tempo of a picture. Originally, motion picture comics went through their paces at breakneck speed as in the Sennett comedies.

Laurel and Hardy also inaugurated in pictures the practice of using their own given names in screen roles. They were for years the foremost practitioners of obtaining a comic effect by inference. That is if Stan pushed Ollie out a window and into a fish pond two stories below, instead of showing a dummy falling out of a window, they would show Laurel pushing Ollie and then cut to Ollie in the fish pond. "The audience conjures a funnier picture in its mind," says Ollie, "then we could possibly show on the screen. The principle of drama is older than the Greek tragedies but for a long while the film industry was so entranced with pictorial scope of the camera that it forgot some of the elemental mechanics of dramatic presentation."

Laurel and Hardy renewing their "Driver's License" sketch. (Frame enlargement)

Another feature of Laurel and Hardy comedy is its complete freedom from anything at all suggestive. Nothing they have ever done in pictures has ever been censored or criticized or put on the "for adults only" list. From time to time they have firmly rejected sequences which undoubtedly would have been screamingly funny because they felt the scenes approached too closely to the border of good taste. In their off-screen conversations the same rule holds true and they never use their talent for fun in a way that would be objectionable to a Sunday School class.

After their contractual troubles and because after a series of unfortunate investments the boys were convinced they were poor business men, they became incorporated. Stan is president, Ollie is vice-president and Ben Shipman, their attorney is secretary-treasurer. Sherman's okay is necessary on any investment they may make. "This way we have to worry first and invest afterwards," says Ollie, with a rueful shake of his head. "It used to be just the other way around with us."

MEASUREMENTS

	LAUREL	HARDY
Height	5 feet 9 in.	6 feet 1 in.
Weight	160 pounds	295 pounds
Hair	Blonde	Brown
Eyes	Blue	Brown

From Howard Strickling
Metro-Goldwyn-Mayer Studios
Culver City, California

BERT LAHR

Thirty-five years of show business have only served to heighten Bert's interest in the theater.

Today he's a seasoned commuter between Broadway and Hollywood. He slips from stage to screen with the facility of long practice. Straight from the starring role in "DuBarry was a Lady," he stepped into a featured spot with Eleanor Powell and Red Skelton in "Ship Ahoy."

Like many another figure in the entertainment world, Lahr was born on New York's East Side. In Yorkville, to be exact, on the 13 of August in 1895. In those days, he was Bert Laehrheim, son of Jacob Laehrheim, interior decorator.

While the other kids went swimming in the East River, Bert spent his time and allowance at the neighborhood theater. It was then he determined to one day be behind those footlights instead of in front of them. At sixteen he organized the "Seven Frolics," made up of kids similarly interested in acting. He actually got bookings for the act. They shared their first bill with none other than Mae West. It was this engagement in a small Texas town, that resulted in a contract with Joe Wood. He dubbed them" "Joe Wood's Nine Crazy Kids." Lahr remained in the juvenile category for some time, then became a vaudeville headliner with "Hardy, Lahr and Usher," which opened at the Brooklyn Olympic Theater. Once again, he and Wood joined forces, and with Jack Pearl formed the "Empire Trio." When Jack Pearl, then top man of the act , took sick, Bert subbed for him, and overnight became a Broadway star. Along with such performers as Fanny Brice, Sophie Tucker, Joe Penner, Jack Haley, Hal Skelly, James Barton, he entered burlesque. The burlesque of those days, in no way paralleled the "strip-tease" shows of today.

After a long and rich career in burlesque during which time he rose from a $35 a week comedian to one of the top-paid performers, Bert came into his own on Broadway's musical comedy stage. His initial chance came in "Delmar's Revels." The show itself was a flop, but not Lahr. It won him the punch-drunk prize fighter role in "Hold Everything," and from then on he was an established star. After it came "Flying High," and his interpretation of the dizzy aviator resulted in his finest screen role when M-G-M made the film version of the Broadway success. He returned to New York for "Hotcha," which also featured Lupe Valez, Buddy Rogers, Lynne Overmann, June Knight and Veloz and Yolanda. In quick succession came "The Show is On," "Life Begins at 8:40," the screen role in "Merry-Go Round of 1938," "Love and Hisses," "Josette," "Just Around the Corner," "Zaza," and then his most important film assignment as the Cowardly Lion in "The Wizard of Oz." He returned to Broadway for "DuBary was a Lady," and now is once again a Hollywood resident for "Ship Ahoy."

Bert Lahr performs as a complaining taxpayer in a frame enlargement from 16mm.

This time he's here for keeps. Of course, he expects to return to the stage at spaced intervals, but at last he has his Hollywood home. It's taken two years to build, but Lahr claims the waiting was worth it. There are two acres of fruit trees, flowers, badminton and tennis courts surrounding his home. It is the one thing that can make Lahr forget that sailing has been his hobby since his days as a gob at the Pelham Bay Naval Training Station. Now he'll devote his time to golf. He shoots a low 80 - - even won the New York Golf Club Championship. He'll also keep up his membership in the Friars Club and the Lambs.

A. M. BOTSFORD
PUBLICITY DIRECTOR
20th CENTURY-FOX
HOLLYWOOD

BIOGRAPHY

of

CHARLOTTE GREENWOOD

Charlotte Greenwood was born in Philadelphia on June 25, 1890, the daughter of Frank Greenwood and his wife, Jacquette Higgins. Miss Greenwood is the wife of Martin Broones, composer and producer.

Educated in the public schools in Boston, Mass., and Norfolk, Va., Miss Greenwood made her made her first appearance on the stage at the New Amsterdam Theater in New York on November 2, 1905, in the chorus of "The White Cat.'

Her first speaking role came as Lola in "The Rogers Brothers in Panama" at the Broadway Theater, September 1907. She subsequently appeared in "The Rogers Brothers in Ireland" and the following year and a small role with Sam Bernard at the Casino in "Nearly a Hero."

Two years in vaudeville followed. She and Eunice Burnham did a pianologue and during the tour Miss Greenwood developed some of the comedy technique that was to prove her stock in trade in later years. She had her first chance to test herself as a comedienne at the Winter Garden in New York in the summer of 1912 when she appeared as Fanny Silly in "The Passing Show of 1912."

In January, 1913, she went into the role of Sodinie in "The Man With Three Wives" at the Weber and Fields theater. Charlotte Greenwood returned to the Schubert fold that July for an important role in "The Passing Show of 1913." She left the show to play the Queen in "The Tik Tok Man of Oz" and in September, 1914, had her first major role, that of Letitia Proudfoot in "Pretty Mrs. Smith."

This engagement led to an association of 8 years under the management of Oliver Morosco. After the tour of "Pretty Mrs. Smith" she appeared briefly in "Town Topics" a New York revue and in the Fall of 1915 came West to go into the all-star production of "So Long Letty."

Before "So Long Letty" had finished its tryout in Los Angeles, Miss Greenwood was topping the cast that included Walter Catlett, Sidney Grand, May Boley, Rock and White, Baldwin and Bronson and many other specialty artists of that day. The company moved East on a triumphant box office march and opened at the Schubert in New York in October, 1916.

While Miss Greenwood really introduced her "Letty" character to America as Letitia Proudfoot in "Pretty Mrs. Smith" it was the Earl Carroll tune, "So Long Letty" that permanently identified her with the character. "So Long Letty" was followed by a series of ""Letty" shows.

Charlotte Greenwood did her eccentric dancing on stage for the Hollywood Victory Caravan. (Frame enlargement)

In November, 1919, at the Fulton in New York, she appeared in "Linger Longer Letty" - in 1921 she made a transcontinental tour as Letty in a musical called "Let 'Er Go Letty" and in the Spring of 1922 she returned to the Vanderbilt in New York in "Letty Pepper."

Miss Greenwood left the Morosco management after this engagement and opened at the Music Box in October, 1922, in "The Music Box Revue." Two years later she was signed by Hassard Short for his "Ritz Revue," an engagement that led to her marriage with Martin Broones.

Hassard Short was having difficulties with a couple of Greenwood numbers and summoned his old friend, Broones. Broones agreed to do two songs for $1000 and to this day Miss Greenwood contends that it would be much cheaper for her to marry the composer. At any rate they were married December 22, 1924, the night the "Ritz Revue" closed in New York.

The show had a long run and a subsequent tour. Broones gave up his London interests to accompany his wife and prepare new material for her. In March, 1927, she opened in New York in Rufus Le Maire's "Affairs." Vaudeville appearances in America and England followed and in 1930, Miss Greenwood tried her hand at straight comedy, without music.

The play was "Mebbe" and in Chicago it had a long and successful run, following a Pacific Coast tryout under the Henry Duffy Management. She subsequently appeared under the joint management of Duffy and Broones in She Couldn't Say No," "She knew What She Wanted," "Parlor, Bedroom and Bath" and "The Alarm Clock."

London first saw her as a musical star in October, 1933, when she appeared at Drury Lane "Wild Violets." It marked the first time an American comedienne had appeared at historic Drury Lane. Miss Greenwood had a long engagement there appearing also as Tiny in "Three Sisters." Later in the Spring of 1934, she went to the Gaiety in London for "Gay Deceivers."

Reminding the audience to buy War Bonds and support the fighting men. (Frame enlargement)

Between the London engagements, Miss Greenwood's career took a strange turn. Convinced that she had talent beyond comedy, she undertook the role as Abby in "The Late Christopher Bean" following Pauline Lord who had played it in New York. Sidney Coe Howard, the author, did not approve of the matter but when he did see the play in San Francisco, paid her the compliment of saying that she was precisely the Abby he had had in mind when he wrote the play.

In December, 1935, Miss Greenwood returned from England to America and started on one of the longest and most profitable tours in the history of the theater with "Leaning on Betsy." she appeared in most of the cities on the United States and was interrupted by the war in Australia on the first leg of a world tour.

On her return from Australia in January, 1940, she was placed under contract by Darryl F. Zanuck of 20th Century-Fox. This was her third career as a film celebrity. She made her first picture in 1918, "Jane." In 1928, after the talkies, she returned to make "Baby Mine," "Girls Will Be Boys," "So Long Letty," "Stepping Out," "Flying High," "Cheaters At Play," "Love Your Neighbor," "Orders Is Orders."

Since 20th Century-Fox, Miss Greenwood has appeared in "Star Dust," "Young People," "Down Argentine Way," "Tall, Dark and Handsome" and "Moon Over Miami."

PICTURE RECORD

"Star Dust"

"Young People"

"Down Argentine Way"

"Tall, Dark and Handsome"

"Moon Over Miami"   424-24

FOR IMEDIATE RELEASE

FROM: ARCH REEVE
HOLLYWOOD VICTORY COMMITTEE
FOR STAGE, SCREEN AND RADIO

Readied by final rehearsals running into the small hours, Hollywood Victory Caravan prepared to take off tomorrow (Sunday, April 26) for its Washington premiere on April 30, 1942.

Twenty-three screen stars, eight starlets and sixty others from the film industry take the three-hour entertainment to twelve of the nation's biggest cities, following the opening in the national capital.

Proceeds of the tour, sponsored by the Hollywood Victory Committee, will be divided equally between the Army Emergency Relief and the Navy Relief Society. The troupe, undoubtedly the most spectacular ever to set off on a tour of big-city one-nighters, was recruited entirely from the film industry by Producer-Director Mark Sandrich and receipts, according to advance advices, are expected to top all previous efforts for the Army and Navy relief cause.

The caravan, under the co-managership of Kenneth Thomson, Chairman of the Hollywood Victory Committee, and Charles Feldman, head of the organization's talent committees, leaves Los Angeles at 12:15 noon Sunday by special train which will be routed direct to Washington.

After the Washington opening the itinerary is as follows: May 1, Boston; May 2, Philadelphia; May 3, Cleveland; May 5, Detroit; May 6, Chicago; May 8, St. Louis; May 9 (afternoon St. Paul; May 9 (evening) Minneapolis; May 10, Des Moines; May 11, Dallas, and May 12, Houston. Final performance will be in San Francisco on a date to be set.

Material for the three-hour entertainment will feature introduction of specially-written sketches and songs supplied by Hollywood Writers' Mobilization headed by Allan Scott. Among the songs introduced will be a new Jerome Kern-John Mercer composition, "Window Under the Sky," to be sung by Frances Langford. Another musical highlight will be the introduction of Rise Stevens of "The Moon is Down," a song poem inspired by John Steinbeck's best-seller and written by Arthur Schwartz and Frank Loesser.

Alfred Newman, one of Hollywood's top musical leaders, will take fourteen of his own men with him to handle the music and will augment this number in each city with a number of local musicians.

Aside from the songs the program will consist of a continuous barrage of comedy sketches and routines, dramatic sketches, whirlwind dance specialties, and spectacular numbers outdoing any variety show that has ever gone on tour.

Bob Hope, in addition to acting as Master of Ceremonies, will have comedy routines with Claudette Colbert and Jerry Colonna, and other comedy spots will feature Joan Blondell, Cary Grant, Charlotte Greenwood, Bert Lahr, Laurel and Hardy, Groucho Marx, and Frank McHugh. Joan Bennett, Charles Boyer, Spencer Tracy, Pat O'Brein, Merle Oberon, Olivia de Haviland and James Cagney will carry the dramatic burden for the show while Desi Arnaz and Ray Middleton handle the male vocal spots opposite Rise Stevens and Frances Langford.

Another of the high spots is a dance line composed entirely of Hollywood starlets, including Katharine Booth, Alma Carroll, Inez Cooper, Frances Gifford, Elyse Knox, Fay McKenzie, Juanita Stark and Arleen Whelan. Topping the dancers will be Eleanor Powell, who has created a special dance routine for the show.

The writers and composers who have supplied material for the show under the sponsorship of the Hollywood Writers' Mobilization include Jerome Chodorov, Matt Brooks, George Oppenheimer, Edward Eliscu, Henry Myers, Julius and Phillip Epstein, George Kaufman, Moss Hart, Martin Berkeley, True Boardman, Joe Shrank, Jay Gorney, Edwin Justus Mayer, Sid J. Perelman, Jerome Kern, John Mercer, Arthur Schwartz and Frank Loesser. Sets were designed by Milt Gross.

With the huge troupe will be a complete staff of executives and aides; including make-up and wardrobe specialists and technicians. Ed Manson will act as transportation manager, Ed Blondell as baggage chief and Dr. Irving Newman as company physician for the tour.

The special train which will take the company direct from Los Angeles to Washington will consist of five sleepers, observation car, diner, parlor car, lounge car and baggage car. A piano is being installed in the lounge car so that rehearsals can continue for the three days on route.

424-23

# # #

THE HOLLYWOOD VICTORY CARAVAN SHOW

The rotation of the acts and content of the Hollywood Victory Caravan changed with each show depending on which stars were present, to tighten up the shows and make the stars happy . As Groucho recalled years later, Laurel and Hardy were a hard act to follow.   Jimmy Cagney also stated how hard it was to follow Bing Crosby. As he recalled in his autobiography, "Fortunately I had some good natural support in the form of my Civil War uniform, eight cute girls, plus 8 American flags blowing in the wind." For many of these stars it was the first time they had met each other. Many permanent friendships were formed.

Audience reaction decided what was expanded on, and what was deleted. Bits and pieces were not only moved around, or eliminated but local pieces were added, like Merle Oberon's reading of a local Soldier's poem in Washington, D.C.

None of the souvenir programs had an order for acts. Even the titles of some of the sketches changed as each city reviewed the show. Songs were changed where appropriate, like the addition of "Deep in the Heart of Texas" for Houston and Dallas.

No single newspaper in any city had a full rundown of what went on during each performance. Reporters generally wrote about what they liked, so it is pretty much impossible to tell, unless specifically mentioned, what played where.

To lessen the repetition, I have listed the stars alphabetically in this chapter. Not all songs and acts were presented in each show, but almost all of them were used on opening night. Keep in mind that the larger the venue, the longer the audience reaction took, creating on the spot eliminations. The show was over four hours long in some cities.

Desi Arnaz - sang and played his conga drum; songs included "Babalu" and "Cuban Pete".

Joan Blondell - performs in "The Ladies", a sketch with Joan Bennett and Olivia de Havilland examining the difficulties of those in high authority engaged in war industries and the raising of the Normandie, from the women's angle, as they take apart a car engine.   Joan Blondell also did a comedy "striptease" with a stuck zipper as a solo.

Joan Bennett - performed in "The Women's Motor Corps" (aka "How To Dismantle An Automobile" or "The Ladies") with Olivia de Havilland and Joan Blondell.

Katherine Booth - one of the starlets that opened the show. Part of the chorus that sang special Arthur Schwartz and Frank Loesser songs, along with some popular musical numbers of the day. Interacted and sang with Bob Hope in the opening, sang and danced behind Groucho Marx and Jimmy Cagney during their numbers.

Charles Boyer - performed a modified version of Alphonse Daudet's "The Last Class", a playlet of defeated France in 1871 with parallels to the present war situation. This was followed by an inspiring tribute to his native France and to America. (He had become an American citizen shortly before the Caravan started.)

Jimmy Cagney - did songs and dances as George M. Cohan in full costume from the movie "Yankee Doodle Dandy." The 8 starlets sang and danced as background. Big numbers were "I'm a Yankee Doodle Dandy," and "You're a Grand Old Flag." Ended the Caravan show with the entire cast singing "God Bless America."

Alma Carroll - one of the starlets that opened the show. Part of the chorus that sang special Arthur Schwartz and Frank Loesser songs, along with some popular numbers of the day. Interacted and sang with Bob Hope in the opening, sang and danced in the chorus behind Groucho Marx and Jimmy Cagney.

Claudette Colbert - enacted "Help Thy Neighbor", with Frank McHugh dealing with the perplexities of an air raid warden confronted by an ardent first aid student. She also participated in a "kissing" routine with Bob Hope, and helped sell a limited number of autographed programs with a kiss to the highest bidder during some intermissions.

Jerry Colonna - swapped verbal quips with Bob Hope, and did a sketch with him called "Life with Mussolini", also did some vocalizing and a trombone solo.

Bing Crosby - who was only in the last 7 shows engaged in banter with Bob Hope, sang "Sweet Leilani," "Miss You," "White Cliffs of Dover" and "Blue of the Night."

Frances Gifford - one of the starlets that opened the show. Part of the chorus that sang special Arthur Schwartz and Frank Loesser songs, along with some popular numbers of the day. Interacted and sang with Bob Hope in the opening, sang and danced behind Groucho Marx and Jimmy Cagney with the full 8 starlets.

Cary Grant - emcee with Bob Hope; did a solo section of jokes aimed each city where the Caravan appeared; performed with Bert Lahr as a shy IRS agent in the "Income Tax" sketch, participated in some intermission auctions with Bob Hope and Claudette Cobert.

Charlotte Greenwood - eccentric dancer and singer, reprising some songs from her movie and stage career, including "Shall I Be an Old Man's Darling or a Young Man's Slave" and "Here Comes the Married Men" from her stage hit "So Long, Letty."

Olivia de Havilland - shared the swing and played "the little woman" who argued with Groucho Marx in the sketch "Where's Olive?" and was also in "The Ladies" with Joan Bennett and Joan Blondell.

Bob Hope - shared the emcee honors with Cary Grant, and did a "kissing" routine with Claudette Colbert. Helped sell a limited number of autographed programs during some intermissions, with Cary Grant, and Claudette Colbert.

Elyse Knox - one of the starlets that opened the show. Part of the chorus that sang special Arthur Schwartz and Frank Loesser songs, along with some popular numbers of the day. Interacted and sang with Bob Hope in the opening, sang and danced behind Groucho Marx and Jimmy Cagney in the chorus.

Bert Lahr - enacted his classic "Song of the Woodsman" which included his wood cutting while his toupee would keep changing positions to comic effect. Also played the part of an unscrupulous highly-paid actor to Cary Grant's shy internal revenue agent.

Frances Langford - sang the newly written Jerome Kern song "Windmill in the Sky."

Stan Laurel and Oliver Hardy - brought their own material, "The Driver License Sketch," from their prior solo personal appearances tours. They were also on stage for "Sweater Boy" and for the finale. The team's theme song, "Dance of the Cuckoos" created show stopping applause whenever played. They had to stand at the microphone and wait for the audience reaction to die down before they could start their routine.

Marie MacDonald - one of the starlets that opened the show. Part of the chorus that sang special Arthur Schwartz and Frank Loesser songs, along with some popular numbers of the day. Interacted and sang with Bob Hope in the opening, sang and danced behind Groucho Marx and Jimmy Cagney in the numbers those stars performed.

Frank McHugh - appeared in "Corregidor" with Pat O'Brien, aka "We'll Be Back," and "Help Thy Neighbor" as an air raid warden opposite Claudette Colbert.

Fay McKenzie - one of the starlets that opened the show. Part of the chorus that sang special Arthur Schwartz and Frank Loesser songs, along with some popular numbers of the day. Interacted and sang with Bob Hope in the opening, sang and danced behind Groucho Marx and Jimmy Cagney with the starlets.

Groucho Marx - worked with Olivia de Havilland in the sketch entitled "Who's Olive"; with Pat O'Brien on "The Barker" where he sang the song "Lydia, the Tattooed Lady;" (eliminated after opening night) and with the starlets as background for his song "Dr. Hackenbush".

Ray Middleton - singer whose songs included "Spread Your Wings" and other current numbers. Normally used with the starlets to close the first half. Also sang "The Son of a Gun Who Picks On Uncle Sam" and a potpourri of military songs and made an appearance in the Cary Grant-Bert Lahr's Income Tax sketch. In Washington, DC, he sang "Keep the Light Burning Bright" to end program with full stage of all actors. On the second chorus, Eleanor Powell came out at the end dressed in red, white and blue, representing Uncle Sam.

Alfred Newman - musical arranger and orchestra conductor for the Hollywood Victory Caravan. Traveled with 14 musicians, and used other locals in each city to expand orchestra. Introduced at end of show along with Mark Sandrich.

Pat O'Brien - presented one of the most dramatic moments of the show by performing "Corregidor" by Jerome Chodorov with Frank McHugh making it clear why the Allied Nations will be victorious ("We'll Be Back"). He followed up with a recitation of the words to "America" to a soft orchestral score, giving new meaning to "My Country 'Tis of Thee." He also did a scene from "Knute Rockne, All-American" and performed an Irish reel and song.

Merle Oberon - performed in "So Long Sam" with Bob Hope, Claudette Colbert, Olivia de Havilland, Groucho Marx, Charles Boyer, Jimmy Cagney and Bert Lahr, in Washington, DC. She also read a poem called "High Flight" written by a pilot killed in action. The musical number was deleted after Washington, DC, but the poem remained in most cities. Her original portion of the show paired her with Spencer Tracy, but had to be eliminated when Tracy could not appear.

Eleanor Powell - tap danced to "Sweater Boy" with the whole male cast, did a solo "Tap for Victory." ("Sweater Boy" was eliminated and "Deep in the Heart of Texas" was added for Dallas and Houston.) Did a tap dancing impersonation of Lt. Jimmy Stewart, who was serving in the Army Air Corp.

Juanita Stark - one of the starlets that opened the show. Part of the chorus that sang special Arthur Schwartz and Frank Loesser songs, along with some popular numbers of the day. Interacted and sang with Bob Hope in the opening, sang and danced behind Groucho Marx and Jimmy Cagney.

Mark Sandrich - was the show's producer. Brought out on stage at the end of the show, and introduced to the audience by Bob Hope.

Rise Stevens - from the Metropolitan Grand Opera sang "Sampson and Delilah," and "The Moon Is Down." Also sang "My Heart At Thy Sweet Voice" from Saint Sean's "Delilah," and "My Hero" " from her picture "The Chocolate Soldier." Stevens added a dramatic touch to her Soprano voice by choosing not to use the microphone on opening night.

Arlene Whelan - one of the starlets that opened the show. Part of the chorus that sang special Arthur Schwartz and Frank Loesser songs, along with some popular numbers of the day. Interacted and sang with Bob Hope in the opening, sang and danced along with the other Caravan starlets behind Groucho Marx and Jimmy Cagney.

WASHINGTON, DC - APRIL 29, 1942

The front cover from the premiere evening of the Hollywood Victory Caravan.

The train was scheduled to arrive at 8:50 in the morning on April 29. Threats of inclement weather did not stop over 4000 movie fans from showing up at Union Station in hope of glimpsing some of their favorite stars. Frances Langford, Olivia de Havilland, Jerry Colonna, James Cagney and Bob Hope arrived later in the day.

Arrival of the largest group of stars ever to converge on Washington, DC. Photo from April 29, 1942 at Union Station by Admiral Arthur J. Hepburn representing the Navy Relief Society.

W7931   WASHINGTON BUREAU
MOVIE STARS ARRIVE IN CAPITOL FOR BENEFIT
WASHINGTON, D.C. HERE'S WHAT THE STAR SPANGLED
TRAIN LEFT HERE WHEN THE MOVIE FOLK PARTICIPA-
TING IN THE HOLLYWOOD VICTORY CARAVAN FOR BENE-
FIT OF ARMY AND NAVY RELIEF SOCIETIES DROPPED
OFF FOR THEIR PERFORMANCE AT THE CAPITOL THEATRE
APRIL 30TH. THE GROUP INCLUDES ADMIRAL ARTHUR
J. HEPBURN, WHO WELCOMED THE STARS, CENTER;
CHARLES BOYER, CLAUDETTE COLBERT, CARY GRANT,
STAN LAUREL AND OLIVER HARDY, BERT LAHR, CHAR-
LOTTE GREENWOOD, ELEANOR POWELL AND OTHERS.
          4/29/42.

Newspaper description affixed to the rear of the photograph above.

Rear Admiral Arthur J. Hepburn shakes hands with Frank McHugh while Claudette Colbert looks on in front of Union Station in Washington, DC.

The "Hollywood Victory Caravan" banner that had to be removed before the train left Los Angeles was again unfurled and hung on the engine. Railroad regulations required its removal when the train was in motion, so it was removed and replaced at each station of the trip. When the train finally arrived at 9:25, the level of the crowd noise increased. Photographers were asked to take their pictures outside the station, but few moved.

Arriving in Washington, DC are Oliver Hardy, Stan Laurel, Juanita Stark, Marie McDonald, and Pat O'Brien.
As the stars became visible, screams of delight and cheers welcomed all. Cary Grant was the first out,

stopping to talk to a friend. Immediately after Grant's exit a member of the Caravan staff announced through one of the train's doors that the stars will be coming out in about 10 minutes.

Joan Bennett was next one out. A few minutes after Bennett, Joan Blondell stepped down. Immediately followed by Claudette Colbert. Then the cascade of stars started. Dressed well, and ready for photographers, they were led down the train platform for the newsreel cameras.

A young male in a grey sports coat had stopped the stars before they went outside. "I don't have to tell you this," he said, "but when you meet the General and the Admiral I want you to be serious, you know, serious."

The music accompaniment was provided by the Army Band. The stars were gathered outside under military protection. Mark Sandrich represented the Caravan and accepted the welcome given by Rear Admiral A. J. Hepburn. The newsreel cameras had to retake their greetings at least twice due to audio issues. All the stars that shook hands with the Rear Admiral had to realign and go through the motions again. Newsreel cameramen from many studios shared footage, and the newsreels were quickly shown in theaters.

Laurel and Hardy are pictured here coming through an honor guard of Army and Navy personnel.

Finally the stars were loaded into jeeps to be taken to the Capitol, then on to the Army and Navy Club for breakfast. A leisurely breakfast was enjoyed, then most stars left to the Willard Hotel, where they were staying for a brief nap. Another rehearsal was scheduled in the Willard hotel at 3 PM.

This rehearsal was similar to the rehearsals that took place on the train as is was staged in sections to separate the acts. Reporters at the time, given a quick tour for publicity, felt it looked like a circus.

As they entered the ballroom, they saw a table off to the side. Sitting at the table were Mark Sandrich, the show's director, and Gene Ford, managing director of the Capitol Theater along with some of his technical people. They were discussing the mechanics of the show. Plotting for sound, lights and scenery had to be finished for the full theater stage rehearsal scheduled for midnight.

Oliver Hardy driving with Stan Laurel in the front, while Rise Stevens, and Eleanor Powell seem amused. Desi Arnaz looks incredulous.

The Historic Willard Hotel, almost unchanged on the outside today. Located at 1401 Pennsylvania Avenue, not far from the White House.

The ballroom as it looked when it was built.

On the other side of the ball room, Jimmy Cagney and Merle Oberon were rehearsing together in one corner. One of the other corners had Olivia de Havilland, Joan Bennett, Joan Blondell and Arleen Whelan going through their bit about women war workers. Upon seeing the reporters being led through, Olivia shouted a hello, and described the routine as "pretty funny."

Just beyond the ballroom was another large room where the musicians were working out the numbers with some of the dancers. One reporter started to open the door to that room, but quickly found it was "off limits" as he just missed being hit in the nose when the door was slammed shut. Occasionally, the door would open as one starlet left after the other - from Elsie Knox, Juanita Stark, Fay McKenzie, Frances Gifford, Inez Cooper, Alma Carroll and Katherine Booth - would drift out. After a short break, all the girls tiredly went back.

A sigh was heard when Claudette Colbert entered the room. Charles Boyer, French by birth, American by naturalization, discussed his last journey on the Ile de France before France's occupation. He told reporters he was going to do a dramatic scene entitled "The Last Class" which was his major contribution to the show. Expressing his concern that "The Last Class" might be too low key for some of the 30,000 seat arenas they were going to appear in, Boyer was still looking forward to his first appearance in front of a live audience. He was also appearing in another sketch called "Sweater Boys."

Press photographers were asked to work with the Caravan to keep all photos as classy as possible. A reporter, having the chance to corner Groucho Marx and Joan Blondell together thought a good gag photo would be to have him leering at her, over his cigar. It looked good to other photographers as well, because a quick crowd gathered. One of the publicity men connected to the caravan stood in front of the pair and calmly reminded the press that they promised not to take any undignified photos. The reporter asked: "How can you take a dignified photo of Groucho Marx?"

Groucho was a great interviewee. Sometimes, even in the 40's the results were not always printable. One of the things he discussed with the reporters was his future Washington D.C. appearance, after the Caravan. It was to be a role in a new comedy. For this show he planned to be a "new" Groucho. As he said "I will be playing it straight, that is, if I'm playing straight right now! No black mustache, no brothers, no frock coat - maybe no audience!"

Groucho poses for some "Leg Art" at the request of a press photographer, comparing his legs to Joan Blondell's. Note Groucho looking dignified with no make-up while Joan Blondell has donned a fresh corsage.

Cagney had gone in to rehearse his dance number. Pat O'Brien, seeing him at rest, called out to him. Oliver Hardy, O'Brien and Cagney left the rehearsal hall. This was just the start of their long day. As the stars had the chance to leave, most tried to catch short naps before the midnight full dress rehearsal on the theater stage. Some of the crew made it back to their rooms by daylight. Most performers figured life would get easier after opening night. At least they could sleep when Washington's final rehearsal ended. Tea at the White House would not be served until late in the afternoon.

WASHINGTON, DC - APRIL 30, 1942

Inside page of Washington, D.C.'s program.

Eleanor Roosevelt at the White House with Hollywood Victory Caravan. Front row, from left: Oliver Hardy, Joan Blondell, Charlotte Greenwood, Charles Boyer, Rise Stevens, Desi Arnaz, Frank McHugh, writer Matt Brooks, James Cagney, Pat O'Brien, Juanita Stark, Alma Carroll. Back row from left Merle Oberon, Eleanor Powell, Arleen Whelan, Marie McDonald, Fay McKenzie, Katharine Booth, Mrs. Roosevelt, Frances Gifford, Frances Langford, Elyse Knox, Cary Grant, Claudette Colbert, Bob Hope, Ray Middleton, Joan Bennett, Bert Lahr, director Mark Sandrich, writer Jack Rose, Stan Laurel, Jerry Colonna, and Groucho Marx.

Mrs. Roosevelt entertained the Hollywood Victory Caravan with a White House tea party, which started around 5:00 PM. All of the stars performing that night had finally arrived in Washington, including Bob Hope and Jerry Colonna. The various colors of the refreshment tents blended nicely with the green of the lawn and the red coats of the Marine Band, present to provide the musical entertainment.

Franklin Roosevelt was occupied by an important meeting in the White House, but during a break, he came to a window and interacted with a few of the stars.

Pat O'Brien and Jimmy Cagney on the White House lawn, with the food tent visible in the background.

Groucho was in normal form during the event. According to Bert Lahr, who tried to be on his best behavior during the event, Groucho was in front of him in the receiving line. Mrs. Roosevelt said "Welcome Mr. Marx, it's a pleasure to have you here." Groucho responded "Why, are we late for dinner?." Bert Lahr was biting his lip so hard to keep from laughing, he never remembered his own introduction to the President's wife.

A general came up to Groucho in the beginning of the event and asked where Mrs. Roosevelt was. His response was "she was upstairs sharpening her teeth." Later in the evening Groucho, in discussing the Marine band turned again to Mrs. Roosevelt and said "Now I know why you travel so much!" Groucho, getting press attention, immediately asked Mrs. Roosevelt about the role of women during the war. Mrs. Roosevelt stated "that not only were women doing some of the men's jobs during their absence, but in many companies, women are running things." Groucho responded, " Well, you're the first woman man enough to admit it!"

The invitation to the White House Tea Party.

Desi Arnaz remembers being impressed with what appeared to be Mrs. Roosevelt's tremendous memory. "Every time anybody came up to her she would say something very personal and very intimate before letting them go by," he said. I know she knew Cary Grant, Charles Boyer, James Cagney, Bob Hope and all the other big stars, but how did she know me and some of the girls who were just starlets? But she treated us all as though we were also big stars.

"When she came to me, she said, 'Hello Desi. How is Lucille?' I was really nobody in those days. So I Was thinking how in hell can she do this?. There were at least 40 or 50 people going by. How can she possibly remember each one, who are they married to, and say something personal to each of them.

"I finally spotted a fellow standing behind her. As she prepared to great us, this guy would whisper to her things like 'Desi Arnaz, married to Lucille Ball, he's a Cuban.' It all happened so smoothly, you never noticed it. I learned how to do this in later years. The next time I came back to Omaha, for instance, it would be impossible for me to remember the names of people I met. I would use Mrs. Roosevelt's technique to make it look like I remembered everyone!"

Lucille Ball was not able to accompany Desi Arnaz on the tour due to her working on the film "The Big Street." She wired her husband and sent her love and greetings to him, and added that their two dogs sent their love to Falla, Roosevelt's dog. When Mrs. Roosevelt read the telegram, she was invited to the White House at a later date. Her dogs Tommy and Pinto were invited as well.

Most of the party ended around 6:30 P. M. because the stars had an 8:30 P. M. curtain, and needed to arrive at the theater in time for their make-up and costumes. Mark Sandrich was the first to leave.

Mrs. Roosevelt, was wearing a black dinner gown of heavy crepe, under a black Mandarin coat with white embroidery when she arrived at the theater. She was accompanied by various ambassadors and visiting dignitaries. NBC was covering the opening, and Mrs. Roosevelt started their radio program by greeting the radio listeners at home. Much of the audience attending the show were military personnel.

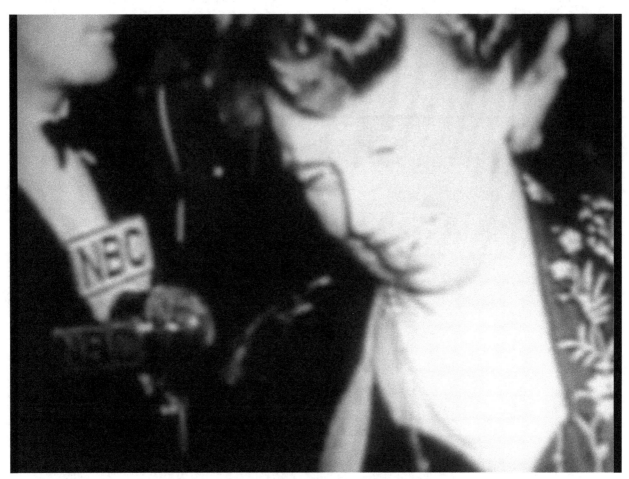

The First Lady speaks on radio at the opening of the Hollywood Victory Caravan as she enters the Capitol Theater. (Frame enlargement)

Loew's Capitol Theater ticket Stub for Thursday April 30.

Desi Arnaz said that he always received top billing over more famous stars when they ran the names alphabetically. His "A" put him on the top of most lists. He was not listed in the ad reproduced above. Bing Crosby was included even though he didn't join the Caravan until Chicago.

The show started on time with Alfred Newman directing the orchestra made up of 14 traveling musicians, and 26 additional musicians from Washington's National Symphony. The opening overture started with "The Star-Spangled Banner." Then the 40 piece group went into "When the Caissons Go Rollin' Along", "Anchors Away" and "The Halls of Montezuma."

The starlets, also known as the "Ladies of the Ensemble," sang an introduction to Bob Hope, who came out and joined them in the last section of the song. He was also the opening emcee. Doing a monologue about the cross country trip that was ahead of him, he then introduced the women to the audience. In Washington, D.C. Desi Arnaz opened the show.

Merle Oberon read a poem called "High Flight." The writer of this poem, R.C.A.F. Pilot John Magee, was local to Washington, DC. He was killed in action in December of 1941. The poetry was read in the Capitol Theater that evening as a dedication to the young man's service. When the boy's father, the Reverend John G. Magee found out it was being read at the theater, he asked if it was being broadcast. Realizing that the minister could not afford a ticket, the Capitol Theater donated two tickets for him and a guest. Mrs. Magee, the Reverend's wife was out of town, so he brought along his younger son, fifteen-year-old Christopher. John Magee's poem received a standing ovation, which lasted for several minutes. There were no dry eyes in the house.

Cary Grant shared the emcee duties, and each act performed beyond the audience's expectations, according to reviews of the time.

The Victory Caravan

Star-Spangled Show for Army, Navy Relief Goes on Before Brilliant Audience Tonight

VICTORY CARAVAN HERE—These seven starlets fresh from Hollywood rehearse the Victory Dance for Army and Navy relief show tonight at Loew's Capitol. They are (from left) Marie McDonald, Juanita Stark, Elyse Knox, Fay McKenzie, Frances Gifford, Alma Carroll and Katharine Booth.

The "Starlets" showing their patriotism by flashing the "V for Victory" sign. An old term, "starlets" appears in this book because it was part of the era, and used throughout the interviews and stories about the Caravan.

Actors Equity Association
American Federation of Radio Artists
Artists Managers Guild
Association of Motion Picture Producers
Independent Publishers Society
Radio Networks

HOLLYWOOD VICTORY COMMITTEE, INC., for stage, screen and radio

Radio Writers Guild
Screen Actors Guild
Screen Directors Guild
Screen Publicists Guild
Screen Writers Guild
Southern California Broadcasting Assn.
Theatre Authority, Inc.

May 1, 1942

Mr. Stanton Griffis
730 Fifth Avenue
New York City, N.Y.

Dear Stanton Griffis:

Thank you for your letter. We are happy that Washington liked the performance so much. We liked Washington.

In your letter you were kind enough to say that we had sacrificed both time and effort. There has been no sacrifice on our part. We know that what we are doing is our duty and obligation.

Because of the nature of the expedition we are fully aware of the difficulties involved. We expect to be pushed around and we will be disappointed a little if we aren't.

We know, too, that what we are doing is a privilege rarely granted to citizens of this country. We are deeply appreciative of the opportunity and our only regret is that we are not playing more cities and towns.

We are proud to be permitted to contribute to this truly noble cause for we are all cognizant of the great sacrificial effort the men in the armed forces are making for all of us, to bring victory -- the victory which we must have -- we will have.

Sincerely,

(Signed/Hollywood Victory Caravan)

Most of the Caravan stars signed a thank you letter to Stanton Griffis. Griffis was the former president of Paramount Studios, a member of Roosevelt's Office of Strategic Services, and chairman of the special events committee for Navy relief for his kind letter praising the performance.

Opening night at the Loew's Capitol had over 3400 attendees, bringing in a total of just under $25,000, below the expected $30,000 that was budgeted. All seats had sold out, and it was not the drawing power of the show that caused the shortfall. Local committees in each city had been set up by the Army and Navy Relief Organization to promote advance ticket sales.

Businessmen, rather than showmen, handled these duties, and it was their lack of experience that hurt the Caravan's gross. In Washington, D.C., the top ticket prices were $20.00. The committee had only sold 60 of these seats in the two week effort before the shows. All other lower price ticket sales were brisk since they were being sold at the Capitol's box office, as well as at hotels and large department stores.

Five dollar tickets sold out immediately, leaving tickets between $7.50 and $20.00 still available. Every effort was put in by local people and businesses to sell every ticket to bring in the largest dollar amount possible. A last minute on-air mention by Walter Winchell helped sell tickets. Since nothing on the scale of the Caravan had ever been attempted before, it was a "learn-as-you-go" experience. The Capitol Theater was the smallest venue they played.

The Caravan ran from 8:30 PM until 12:20 AM on opening night and was accompanied a constant stream of applause. The Caravan had none of the major rough spots expected on a first night. Considering the revue's size, the fact that it was quickly assembled, and only briefly rehearsed, it was a good omen of things to come.

All were back on the Victory Caravan train by 2:00 AM, and heading for Boston, their second stop.

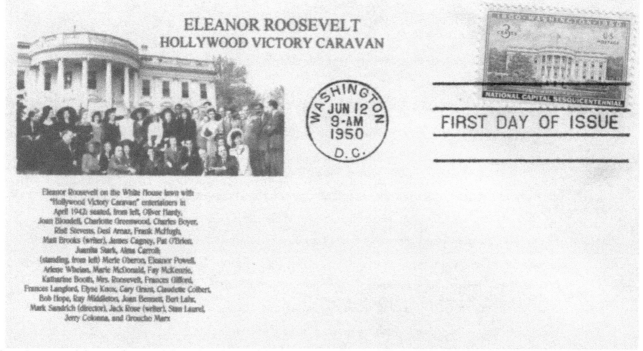

First day issue of the 150th year of the White House. The Hollywood Victory Caravan left such a lasting impression that it was recalled 18 years after the event.

WASHINGTON, D.C. - "To Babe"

Oliver Hardy was know by his family, co-workers, and loved ones by the name of "Babe". Many years ago, Hardy had gone to an older barber who, as he finished Hardy's shave would pat his cheeks and say "You're okay, baby!" The name Babe stuck, and in early films, he was known as Babe Hardy, or Oliver "Babe" Hardy.

The photos in this chapter are reproduced from his personal copy of the opening night Souvenir program. The full color cover, pictured earlier shows a store window display of Army and Navy uniforms while a little child looks in on the display. The child has two toys dragging behind him, representing both branches of the service.

The meaning of the "quips" inscribed are lost to history. It's like reading someone's High School Yearbook. We weren't there, and except for the obvious straightforward signings, we will probably never know what the inside jokes were about.

To "Baby" I like you too! Sincerely Desi. Notice the misspelling of "Arnez"

Dear Oliver it was really grand to make this trip with you - and to become your friend!
Charles Boyer

To my li'l pet Babe ----- Wherever he finds a corner I'll be in it!   Jim

To Babe ----- Success and happiness to you always   Claudette

To "Babe" With sincerest admiration to a great guy and a great actor   Your friend always   Jerry Colonna

To Ollie whose presence made the tour terrific ----- Bing Crosby

To Dear Babe ----- with warm and fond wishes -- and many memories. Cary.

To Mr. Hardy My especial and Bestest Pal --- on the Caravan   always Charlotte Greenwood
Babe - It's a great privilege to know you!! Martin Broones
(Charlotte Greenwood's husband)

My love always old Hardy!   _Stan_

MR. BERT LAHR

To My Doll Boy "Babe"   I love you dear   Bertram

GROUCHO MARX

To Babe --- The prettiest grey-hound bus I have ever seen --- fond Memories   Groucho.

To Oliver, and our wives are friends, too! All the best in the world to you. Yours Sincerely- Frank McHugh "Air Ward Raiden"[sic]

Affectionately inscribed to Babe Hardy with the admiration of <u>Ray Middleton</u>

To my lovely victim   Long may you be in my power.   Your Satanic Pal Pat

To "Babe" You are a loveable person and I sure are fond of you - Don't forget your Victory partner Eleanor Powell.   Dated 5/1
Best Wishes Always - Mother Powell (Eleanor Powell's mother traveled with her.)

To "Babe" A very grand person. I will treasure knowing you. Rise Stevens
To "Babe" I am very proud to know you.   -- Walter Surovy (Rise Steven's Husband)

WASHINGTON, D.C. - "To Charles Boyer"

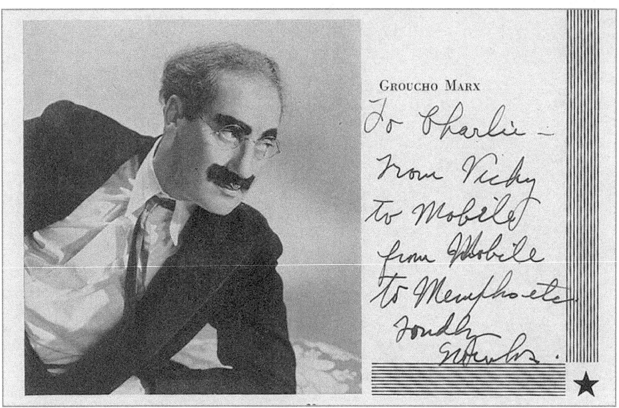

"To Charlie - From Vichy to Mobile from Mobile to Memphis etc.   Fondly Groucho."

BOSTON, MASSACHUSSETES - MAY 1, 1942

The Statler Hotel (now the Boston Park Plaza Hotel) had been preparing for days for the Hollywood Victory Caravan's arrival in Boston. There was a heavy police guard placed at the hotel. The entire sixth floor was turned over to the Caravan as the Statler's donation to the cause. The advance agents from the Caravan had helped the hotel set up for what was promised to be the biggest extravaganza in Boston's history. Long lists of arrangements had to be made for the protection of the stars from well meaning fans, whose sheer numbers posed many logistical issues. The stars even had a separate elevator which was barred from other guests.

Opened in 1927, the Statler Hotel as it appeared in the 40's from a vintage linen post card. At the time of the Hollywood Victory Caravan, it was the largest hotel in New England and the eighth largest in the world.

All the local newspapers were dedicating page after page to help maximize the exposure of the Caravan. One of the major tasks was to get 100 volunteers to act as drivers and transport the Caravan from the hotel to the Boston Garden for the performance. Under normal circumstances, new car dealerships would have provided cars in return for the publicity, but this was wartime, and automobile stock was frozen. Only people with open top cars could apply. Thousands of applications were received, many from Harvard, Dartmouth, and Tufts Universities. Some volunteers requested specific stars, with Olivia de Havilland having had the most requests.

It was decided to have a random drawing for the 100 drivers needed. The Civil Defense Center committee went through each letter to select the newest of the cars offered that were also the most comfortable. Similarly, genuine film fans have been given preference in the final choosing of entries. Instead of the normal fishbowl, the names were drawn from a land mine and announced. The order of the drawing decided which person drove which star.

Charles "Buddy" Rogers and Patsy Kelly were appearing in person at the RKO Boston Theater and had arranged their show schedule to draw the names. The drawing was held at 12:30 PM the afternoon of April 25th outside the Boston Post Newspaper Building. Thousands watched as the names were drawn. In an interview over 40 years later, "Buddy" Rogers remembered that afternoon and said it was "his honor to contribute in any way to the American cause." He also recalled that the land mine had been salvaged from enemy waters, and was not one of our own.

Chosen drivers had each received identification badges and had to report to the meeting site, Columbus Avenue from the Berkley Street side that evening. The parade routes were being planned to give the largest possible amount of exposure to the stars.

"The Star Spangled Special" was originally scheduled to pull into the South Street Station. In order to reduce the crowds, and provide a measure of security, it was decided to stop the train at an undisclosed location. The short parade from the station to the hotel that was originally scheduled that morning was cancelled. Wishing to empty the train of the recognizable stars, it turned out that only the stars that needed the rehearsal time left the train. The rest remained.

Patsy Kelly and Buddy Rogers Will Draw Cars for the Hollywood Caravan Next Friday

BUDDY ROGERS AND PATSY KELLY HERE

Charles "Buddy" Rogers and Patsy Kelly cross their fingers to bring luck to the drawing entries.

The train finally arrived around 10:30 AM. The people remaining on the train slowly trickled out as they woke up. First off the train were Stan Laurel, Oliver Hardy, and Charlotte Greenwood.

First off the train were Stan Laurel, Charlotte Greenwood and Oliver Hard, shown in this old newspaper clipping.

Two hundred uniformed military police lined both sides of the train. Police Superintendent Edward T. Fallon and his officers tried to keep the people on the platform at a minimum. Three thousand people eventually made it into the station, with another estimated 20,000 waiting outside for a glimpse of the stars leaving the train and getting into the waiting cars. There was a line of waiting automobiles to take the stars directly to the Statler Hotel as they left the train. Fans cheered each star as the appeared. It took a "flying wedge" of 50 soldiers to move each small group of celebrities through the crowds to their cars to the Statler where they had time to freshen up before the parade.

Jacqueline Ligham of Roxbury nails up a poster at Civilian Defense Center in Boston.

After the stars had rested a bit, they worked their way down to the lobby and made time for interviews and photos before going to their cars. Most of the questions asked at the hotel were light-hearted comments, keeping with the patriotic occasion.

Cary Grant was rumored to be romantically linked with Barbara Hutton, the Woolworth heiress. During this time period, she used her high-profile image to sell War Bonds. She received positive publicity after being derided by the press as a result of her marriage scandals. Married twice before, Grant was to be husband number three in July of 1942, less than two months after the Caravan. At the time, their actual plans were not publically known, and the press mentioned the couple as "Cash and Cary."

A female reporter shouted out "What's the answer to you and Barbara Hutton?" Without blinking an eye, Grant responded with "There ain't no answer," followed with "No quotes!" The reporter said to him "too late, it's already gone 'round the world." Reporters speculated if Grant has proposed yet, or if Hutton had not accepted yet. Although the reporter who asked the question was given a cold shoulder, almost every newspaper used the quotes in their stories. Even the songwriter Martin Broomes (husband of Charlotte Greenwood) liked Grant's reaction so much, he wanted to use "It Ain't No Answer" as a song title.

Charles Boyer was another of the leading men that were popular with the ladies. He spent time walking around, and sat for a while with Merle Oberon and Joan Blondell. Even among the famous, he had such varied parts, that without make-up, he just appeared "ordinary." A man waiting to talk to Joan Blondell asked who the man was that was sitting with her. When told it was Boyer, the man thought he was at the receiving end of a joke.

Boyer told Blondell "There's a terrible crowd downstairs," referring to the size. He continued, "I must say they were well behaved. It is Boston, I'm told." Overhearing that Boyer was upset about not being recognized, she told the crowd, "Boyer is such a great artist on the screen that no one recognizes him off the screen. That's a tribute. We American's have those frank, matter-of-fact faces that can be spotted a mile off in any crowd."

Groucho Marx, one of the world's most well known comedian, was also not recognized in this crowd without his customary screen make-up. While he wasn't overly fond of being ignored, he also had a sense of humor about it. He would move among the crowd asking "Have you seen the movie stars?" One of the fans looked him straight in the face and replied, "Yes, but we are looking for that funny guy, Groucho. Where is he?"

Since it was war time, it had been suggested by the government to put a ceiling on higher salary earners, with all pay not to exceed $25,000 a year. James Cagney, who's newest contract gave him approval to set up his own production company, said it made little difference. "If this thing (the war) goes sour, what have you got left anyway? Hollywood won't resent a cut in salaries if it is necessary to the war effort. Most of them would gladly accept it, and there would be little grousing about it." Cagney added that he had a farm in Martha's Vineyard and a small house in Hollywood which cost less than $25,000 to maintain, and it "was enough for any man." Pat O'Brien agreed.

Joan Bennett thinks that a $25,000 salary would require some sacrifices. In anticipation, she had dismissed her studio maid and bought fewer clothes.

Interviewed together, Cary Grant, Charlotte Greenwood, and Claudette Colbert also stated they expected no change in their lifestyles. "The $25,000 a year for personal spending will simplify life all around. I'm all for it. I shall not have to change my life in the least." Charlotte Greenwood replied: "Let them close up a section of the house and live in a few rooms. One maid is all any movie star should have and if we don't work, well, we can do our own housework, like the women of England. Women in England who have had many servants are now doing their own cooking; and why not!"

When asked, Merle Oberon said: "Unfortunately, I have a big house and I shall have to make some adjustments."

Much of the discussion was about the hardships of traveling. Despite the fatigue of touring, the female half of the show looked like they were fresh from a movie set. While some were immediately recognizable, some had personalities that made them look better in person, while some had minor defects hidden by the camera.

Rise Stevens and Eleanor Powell were reported to be "brimming over with genuine friendliness" and "have a sparkling personality which doesn't show in the characters they portray in a film."Rise Stevens, tall and well built, was the first female in the "press room." She wore a navy-blue outfit accented with Kelly green and a mink coat. Her ensemble was topped off with a slanted straw bonnet and veil. Eleanor Powell wore no hat over her dark red hair. Her gold colored summer silk dress was worn under a three-quarter lynx coat.

Frances Langford's bright blue dinner skirt was coupled with a white and blue print blouse. Her bright blonde hair contrasted well with her grey cloth coat with fur trim. Joan Blondell, slightly heavier than her usual film appearance, wore a hooded dress in black with print trimmings.

The starlets Elyse Marks, Katharine Booth, Alma Carroll, Frances Gifford, and Arleen Whelan - seemingly immune to the full Hollywood trappings - wore simple bright colored suit dresses. Charlotte Greenwood wore a mink jacket over a brown silk dress with a fully pleated skirt.

While most stars wore "glamorous" make-up, Joan Bennett looked almost pale in comparison. With just a touch of lipstick, and letting her hair go back to its natural brown, she looked more like "the girl next door" than most. Her dress was a black silk one, with a floral design, topped with a silver fox jacket.

Starting with Cary Grant, the Caravan Stars made their way out to the waiting cars at 4:00 PM for the parade to the Boston Gardens.

Mounted police were positioned throughout the parade route, while a full squadron of motorcycle police led the parade. Lining the streets were an estimated one million people. The applause and shouting that started in the hotel lobby followed throughout the tour. Military Police stood shoulder-to-shoulder holding back the crowd, as the stars emerged from the Statler and went to their cars. Shouts of "That's Cary Grant" barely faded when Boston-born Jerry Colonna followed in the second car out. Each car carried an identifying plaque.

Claudette Colbert surprised people by how tiny she appeared. When Laurel and Hardy drove by the applause grew. Bert Lahr stated that city after city the noise would drop as he went by, since he did not have a large movie career and was not as recognizable as the others. His biggest film up to that point had been in heavy make-up as the Cowardly Lion in MGM's "The Wizard of Oz." When a bigger star came up behind him, the crowd would again regain its volume.

Each star was assigned two soldiers to ride with. The soldiers would hold the star in place, as they sat on the folded roofs of the convertibles. When Joan Blondell took her seat, one of her escorts, Private Alfred Taddea took hold of her waist. He asked if Joan Blondell would give him an autograph. Blondell said loudly, "Of course, Private," and as she did, the crowd roared its approval.

It was noticed that Eleanor Powell's service men were blushing a bit, but she soon put them at ease as the parade continued. She commented to her mother riding along with her: "Listen to that! Doesn't that make it worthwhile to be a star?" The crowds loved Powell, who was also Massachusetts born.

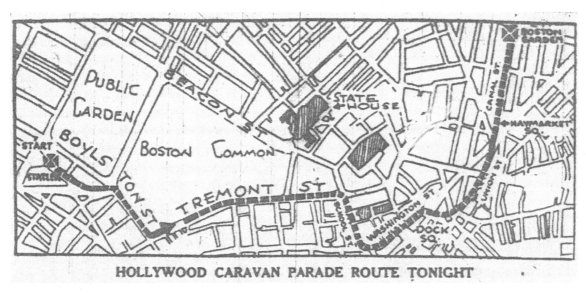

HOLLYWOOD CARAVAN PARADE ROUTE TONIGHT

The Parade route.

Charlotte Greenwood, riding car number 13, waved enthusiastically, as her character on film and stage would have. It made her extremely visible to the people hanging from windows, and those standing on roof tops. Workers stayed beyond their workday to retain access to these windows.

Slightly jealous of the responses, Groucho probably resented being unrecognized without his greasepaint. He eventually ended up walking alongside his car, making funny comments to the crowd. Still most movie fans did not recognize him.

Every available spot along the parade route was occupied. A young boy, William Prince, was watching the parade from a tree in the Boston Common. In his excitement, he lost his balance and fell 30' through the skylight at the Boylston Street entrance. Taken to city hospital he had a concussion, dislocated hip and cuts to his face. This appeared to be the only accident along the route.

Boston's Mayor Tobin rode with Pat O'Brien. Since Bob Hope was late returning from lunch, he joined the parade in the last car. When Hope's car passed through, the applause hit its height, and women held their small children high so they could see the "Pepsodent Peddler" as Variety had named him. James Cagney was also one of the crowd's favorites, and the women in the crowd drew forward to see Desi Arnaz better.

The parade was scheduled to travel at 30 miles-per-hour. Some streets were so jammed with people the cars slowed down to 5 mph, and had to stop numerous times until the streets were cleared enough for the parade to continue.

Observed in the crowd waiting outside at the Boston Garden end of the parade were "look-a-likes." There were at least three "Joan Blondells," three "Claudette Colberts," and two "Myrna Loys," (who wasn't even a part of the Caravan) spotted.

Frances Langford waves to the crowd during the parade.

There was a brief time between the stars arrival and the show, so musical numbers were rehearsed to bring up the local musicians and lighting and sound checks were performed on the singers and performers to test the systems in use before "curtain" time.

The day of the performance only 80% of the tickets were sold. By the 8:30 curtain time, all seats and standing room were sold out to over 20,000 people.

It had been announced about two weeks prior to the show that more than six thousand box locations had already been subscribed and the full capacity of 1500 single seats will be sold out prior to opening day. These tickets were priced from $1.10 to $11.00. Two thousand additional "standing room only" tickets were sold at $2.20 each.

Learning from the first show, tickets were sold by all theaters, as well as at Filene's and Jordon Marsh Stores and at the Boston Garden itself. The Boston local committees had done a much better job, having used 25 local press agents rather than the city's businessmen for promotional efforts. With a goal of $75,000 the Boston Garden show ended up filling over 20,000 seats and taking in $77,750.

Section D Row 4 Seat 7/8 on the floor of the Boston Garden, placed into a copy of the Souvenir Program for May 1st. $7.70.

Another old clipping, this time of D. B. Stanbro of the Hotel Statler as he purchased a block of tickets for the Boston show. Selling the tickets are Marian Gabriel and Marylyn Nichols. Note the photo of Spencer Tracy to the right of the poster. His inability to appear had not been known when this photo was taken. Interestingly enough, the photo they are holding is a portrait of Laurel and Hardy.

From a linen postcard. The interior of the original Boston Garden, which held over 20,000. Stage was center end, placed in the area under the flag visible in postcard against the fixed seats.

Banner above the makeshift stage read: "Motion Picture Industry - Hollywood Victory Caravan" Floor seats were configured to face the stage. Actors turned during performance to address the patrons seated in the stadium seating behind the stage.

The show started on time, but about 30 minutes were cut from the original Washington, DC show. The show ran much "tighter" and went over with the audience and reviewers alike.

One of the unique differences in Boston was the audio equipment. Unforeseen mechanical difficulties made the show funnier at times. Fully tested before the show, the microphones that had been set up did not carry the sound over the crowd. Bob Hope was given a hand microphone, and extras, some on stands were placed at the front of the stage for the sketches and singers.

The crowd was not shy in expressing their disapproval. Since many of the bits were dependant on hearing the actors, shouts of "louder" and "turn up the sound" ran through the audience all evening. Groucho and de Havilland's "Where's Olive?" had to stop and restart three times, finally with hand held microphones.

Dramatic sketches had to be accommodated to microphones for which they were never designed for. Boyer's serious presentation became an anachronism when he held the mike in his 1870 classroom.

The press noted that it gave Bob Hope and Cary Grant the chance to ad-lib all evening. Bob Hope was used to impromptu responses, and Cary Grant held his own. In a later interview, Groucho remarked that Bob Hope traveled with a team of writers. When he heard that Hope's material was only prepared by six of his writing staff, he quipped, "For Hope, that's ad-libbing!"

Claudette Colbert, Bob Hope and Cary Grant added another $1750 by auctioning off 3 autographed copies of the night's program, one each. Top dollar went for Colbert's copy. Hers sold at the $1000, and came with a kiss for the highest bidder, local liquor wholesaler Al Benjamin. A "flying squadron" of military police and regular officers escorted Colbert right into the stands. She kissed Benjamin, who by this time had a red face, as flash bulbs popped and the crowd roared in approval.

Olivia de Havilland and Groucho Marx hold their microphones while performing their "Where's Olive" segment.

Actual film footage of the Hollywood Victory Caravan's performance is rare. In Boston this home movie shows Cary Grant, Bob Hope, Joan Blondell, and Cary Grant. Captured by a soldier's camera, it shows a good portion of Greenwood's dance and Bondell's strip tease.

Frame blow-up of rare home movie taken in Boston Gardens. Charlotte Greenwood on stage starts her number. The original microphone visible on the floor in the lower left of the picture did not function properly, so several standing mikes were added to the stage. (Frame enlargement)

Frame blow-up of Charlotte Greenwood on stage at the Boston Garden starting her famous high kick.......

.....and at the height of it, with her foot higher than her head. (Frame enlargements)

Blondell's "Striptease" starts as Cary Grant slowly backs offstage after his introduction.

Blondell's zipper becomes stuck......

......and she has no shortage of help as Bob Hope tries to prove. (Frame enlargements)

During this night's performance, James Owen Cherry, Interstate Circuit's city manager of Dallas theaters flew out from Texas to preview the show his city would host on the 11th. Joining him was Mayor Tobin of Boston and R. J. O'Donnell, the vice president of the Interstate Circuit. Cherry was quoted as saying, "I've been in show business a long time, but the way the Caravan stood staid old Boston on its dignified head was one of the most amazing things these old eyes have ever seen.

"People lined the streets from five in the afternoon until midnight to catch a glimpse at the stars, who paraded in open cars, with a deafening roar when they went by. Backstage the stars acted like a bunch of kids on a holiday, ribbing each other and cheering the other fellow's act.."

He asked Cary Grant why he and others were teary-eyed during the parade. Grant put it this way: "It did something to me inside. It dug right down into the pit of my stomach to see such appreciation!" Cherry responded with "If you think this is hospitality and enthusiasm, just wait until you are deep in the heart of Texas. Then you'll see some."

The only complaint heard was from Groucho Marx. Probably still a bit envious of the recognition the other stars received, he complained about what he thought was the scarcity of humor in his and de Haviland's "Where's Olive?" sketch. "What's wrong? You don't see Hope complaining?" said Sandrich. Groucho said that "it was all right for guys like Hope. He has over a dozen writers to help him with his material."

Sandrich corrected him. "Hope has only six writers" he said, "and the only reason he has them along is because he is also doing his radio show while we are on the road." Groucho looked at Sandrich, and with his normal style of delivery said "Six writers! For Hope that's practically ad-libbing!"

When all was said and done, the audience felt like part of the show. The troupe headed back to the train. At the station were over 200 people seeking autographs. The military guard prevented access to the stars, to keep order and protect the Caravan troupe. The train left at 2 AM for Philadelphia.

Charlotte Greenwood attended school in Boston and Jerry Colonna was born in Boston. Here they share a pot of traditional Boston Baked Beans.

PHILADELPHIA, PA - MAY 2, 1942

Original souvenir program for the Philadelphia performance. Cover art by John Falter.

The train carrying the stars was shunted to a siding at 30th Street Station, to let the stars rest. About quarter to one it was pulled into another siding to allow the hairdressers and manicurists one more chance to put the final touches on hair and nails. Then the train was backed into the Broad Street Station at Market Street, to utilize the train platform as a stage for the stars. Over 700 fans lined the platform, behind its gates. With the constant announcements of a sold out show, many people knew this would be the only glimpse they would have of the stars.

The late arrival was a disappointment to the fans that waited since 9 AM, when the train was scheduled to pull in. Since the personalities were still on the train during lunch hour, the crowd in front of the gates grew to become thousands, stretching the "unofficial" welcoming party the entire route to the hotel.

Policemen linked arms and strained back against the pressing crowd. A one point, the fans broke through and started down the platform toward the train, but they were moved back. Railroad brakemen and office workers had a view from balconies under the train shed. The stars started their exit from the train in small groups, each one appearing to thunderous applause.

At this station, the first to step out were Claudette Colbert, and Oliver Hardy. Hardy, ever the gentleman, grinned broadly to the crowd, and remarked that it was a case of "beauty and the beast." Claudette was wearing a black dress and a close-fitted little pink hat with two large rosebuds and a voluminous tulle veil caught under her chin. No one mistook her for Stan Laurel!

Stan Laurel had gone down the train steps when a policeman stopped him and asked him to go back until a path could be made to get him through the crowd. He did his trademark cry to the delight of the fans, and did as he was asked. Groucho also started out thinking he was normally not recognized without his stage make-up. He returned as well when couldn't see a way to get through the crowd.

The police finally created an open path through to the Filbert Street train exit, where cars were waiting to take the stars to the hotel. Mingled in with the drivers were many young women from the Navy League (Nells) who drove as escorts of honor.

MOVIE STARS AS THEY ARRIVED HERE FOR HOLLYWOOD VICTORY CARAVAN SHOW
Some of the motion picture stars who arrived here yesterday for the Hollywood Victory Caravan show staged last night at Convention Hall are shown above at Broad Street Station. Among those in the picture you may identify Cary Grant, Charles Boyer, Claudette Colbert, Merle Oberon, Charlotte Greenwood, Pat O'Brien, James Cagney, Groucho Marx, Frank McHugh, Eleanor Powell, Stan Laurel, Bert Lahr and Arleen Whelan. They were welcomed by 25,000 fans. Their tour is for the benefit of Army and Navy relief.

Newspapers of the day built up the excitement!

122

Shortly before 1 PM the others came out, exiting through the train platform. Most people stopped to wave as they left the train. Merle Oberon, wearing a simple pink dress with a black dot in the print, and a black hat with pink dots in the veil, was the next one out. She was followed by Olivia de Havilland, who wore a black dress, with a wide brimmed felt hat trimmed with straw, and a Persian lamb cape. Claudette Colbert, in a black dressand pink hat was followed by Frances Langford, who's outfit was Kelly green.

Following right behind were Joan Blondell, Joan Bennett, Eleanor Powell, Rise Stevens, and Charlotte Greenwood. Jimmy Cagney, Jerry Colonna, Charles Boyer, Cary Grant, Bert Lahr and Pat O'Brien were the last to exit the train. As Pat O'Brien stood on the platform, he was formally greeted by the Notre Dame Club of Philadelphia who presented a plaque to him for his role in the Warner Brothers' movie "Knute Rockne". Missing was Bob Hope, who stayed in Boston to get some additional sleep. He arrived by airplane and went straight to the hotel.

The crowds were amazing in the restraint and cooperation they gave the police. Although loud, there were no incidents going to the hotel. Most of the work that day came from holding back the photographers, both professional and amateur. Since most of the stars came out late, there was a line of people from the station to the hotel estimated at 25,000. The street was closed off in front of the hotel.

At the hotel, fans tried all kinds of methods get a look at, or a word to their favorite star. Hundreds of calls swamped the hotel switchboard, while fans presented themselves at the front desk as a long lost relative.

The Ritz-Carlton was one of the hotels that picked up the cost of the Caravan's food and lodging as part of their contribution to the war effort. The only real item of expense to the Hollywood Victory Caravan's budget was the cost of the railroading, which had to be paid according to Federal Law.

On Sunday afternoon, Old Famous Bookbinder's Restaurant had a special menu consisting of Steamed Lobster, Philadelphia Potatoes and War Bond Salad. Bob Hope had wanted to eat at this landmark restaurant. Given a table toward the back, he received his drink and bread, and was just starting his meal.

Huge crowds formed outside Bookbinder's restaurant Seeing the hundred or so people gathered outside, Hope left his table and went into the crowd with a bread basket. Keeping up an impromptu flow of short jokes he proceeded to toss the bread into the fans. Before going back in, he thanked everyone for the support received and passed the empty breadbasket to gather a contribution from the people there.

Hedda Hopper's daily column publicized the Hollywood Victory Caravan. "There are no flies on Cary Grant. During the Victory Caravan Tour, he's had a newsreel camera following him….and the Caravan has been proving all over again what I've been howling about, that some of our greatest entertainers don't get a chance here until the public outside howls for them….and Hollywood better have some nice fat parts for them or their fans will be yodeling again."

Cary Grant took an automobile trip through the Main Line, explaining he wanted to see it ever since making "The Philadelphia Story", which was a story about the Main Line. He was followed the entire trip by newsreel cameramen. Grant announced that this newsreel footage would be used in an upcoming film "Bundles for Freedom" to be made by RKO, his current studio. Released in May of 1943, the title had changed to "Mr. Lucky" and featured Cary Grant, Charles Bickford and Gladys Cooper.

By the morning of May 2nd, announcements on radio and in the newspaper were calling for restraint on the part of fans. Thousands had waited too late to make their purchase, and were turned away with the curt statement that "the house was sold-out to the 'last square foot." With only 13,500 available seats, 16,000 tickets were sold, utilizing all possible standing room, for a grand total of $31,500.

Pleas were issued that those not possessing tickets remain away from the Convention Hall, because there were no tickets available. It was felt that the presence of added thousands of people outside might create great confusion.

Bookbinder's special Hollywood Victory menu.

Philadelphia followed Boston's lead with more affordable prices. It sold to standing room only.

With successful reviews, the Philadelphia show went just slightly over the three hours predicted. The show had become smoother since its premier and, with the 16,000 paid admissions, the box office took in $31,500, more than Washington, D.C. but about 40% of Boston's total.

Philadelphia War Memorial Coliseum

About seven minutes of silent Kodachrome 16mm home movie footage, shot from the audience, still exists of the evening's performance. For what the Hollywood Victory Caravan footage looks like, frame blowups were used earlier, interspersed throughout the press book pages in the third chapter of this book, as well as in this chapter. With all home movies done with film, if you couldn't use a tripod, or steady the camera, you ended up with a soft focus. Not visible as much when being shown as a movie, the focus becomes more visible when you look at the actual frames.

The person who filmed this back in 1942 had owned a three lens camera, so some shots are long, medium and close-up. Only the best individual frames were chosen for reproduction. It appears to be the longest recording of the Caravan show found., and the only footage in color.

Inside the Philadelphia War Memorial Coliseum just before the lights dimmed and the show started.

Admiral Arthur J. Hepburn, representing the Navy Relief Society, who traveled with the Caravan opened the show with the only solemn speech of the evening. "In this globe-encircling war, many forces had to be mobilized," he said. "The Hollywood force, represented here tonight by many of its foremost actors and actresses - a force which is ever alert, eager and ready to volunteer in the service of this country - is touring the leading cities of America for the benefit of the two service relief societies." Receiving a standing ovation, he left the stage and the spotlight went dark.

Admiral Arthur J. Hepburn opens the show. (16mm frame enlargement)

Alfred Newman directed a 70 piece orchestra on the coliseum's rising stage. The overture started, and the audience stood while the Star Spangled Banner played. As well as the orchestra carried through the coliseum, the singing of the audience was as loud as the instruments.

A 16mm frame blow-up of four of the eight starlets opening the show.

When the stage lit again, the eight starlets(Katherine Booth, Alma Carroll, Frances Gifford, Elyse Knox, Fay McKenzie, Marie McDonald, Juanita Stark, and Arleen Whelan) did the opening number of the evening. One of the songs they sang before Bob Hope came out was about wartime clothing shortages.   They sang:

> "They took away our girdles, and silk stockings are taboo.
> Nobody bought us mink this year the way HE used to do.
> But we're gonna break the axis if we have to break it naked;
> For Victory - we can take it!"

Joining the women, Bob Hope finished the last song with them, and welcomed the audience. Using topical humor along with local the show was off to a flying start. A huge round of applause greeted Hope's mention of Manayunk, a nearby city. He introduced the starlets by name, and as they left the stage, Hope quipped "Boy! Look at this Crowd - am I packin' 'em in!" The audience roared, and Hope added: "That's the kind of girls I work with. You ought to see the kind I get."

Another frame shot as Bob Hope interviewed one of the starlets before going into his monologue. (16mm frame enlargement)

Star after star came on, sang, danced, told jokes, and enacted broad farce and straight drama. First up was Desi Arnaz and his "Cuban Pete" number. He did a number of songs, providing his own conga drum beat.

Desi Arnaz at the microphone. (16mm frame enlargement)

Next up were Olivia de Havilland and Groucho Marx with a bit of "pun" comedy. Cary Grant came out for his introduction as co-master of ceremonies. After a brief give and take, Grant took over Hope's role. The three hour show needed two mc's. Grant introduced Joan Blondell, who did her "Burlesque Striptease."

Olivia de Havilland and Groucho Marx perform in "Where's Olive", one of the first farce comical moments. (16mm frame enlargement)

Cary Grant takes over for Bob Hope. Grant, a British citizen at the time of the Caravan became a naturalized American citizen on June 26, 1942. (16mm frame enlargement)

Joan Blondell comes out onto the stage. (16mm frame enlargement)

Joan Blondell starts her "hard boiled" stripper number. (16mm frame enlargement)

Joan Blondell, before the sticking zipper that prevented her from finishing her striptease. (16mm frame enlargement)

Running off stage to avoid Bob Hope and Groucho Marx's help. (16mm frame enlargement)

After being chased off the stage, Joan Blondell returns to take her bows. (16mm frame enlargement)

Charlotte Greenwood stopped the show when she came out, as did Laurel and Hardy as the show built to toward its intermission. Bob Hope announced Claudette Colbert and gets involved in a conversation about the spreading custom of selling kisses with war bonds to increase sales. He gets Claudette to go along with the idea, and gets his kiss - and a second one. - and a third. Stopping the kissing, Claudette looked toward the audience and said: "I hope the Army and the Navy appreciate what I'm doing for them!" and walked off the stage. Bob Hope announces intermission as the orchestra started up. The coliseum lights slowly rose as the orchestra finished their rendition of the theme song for the Caravan written by Jerome Kern and Johnny Mercer called "Windmill in the Sky." The first half of the show was over.

Charlotte Greenwood taking in the standing ovation she received. (16mm frame enlargement)

The expressions on Laurel and Hardy's faces tells all as they start their Driver's License routine, another show stopper. (16mm frame enlargement)

Laurel explains that his license has "perspired," while Hardy listens. (16mm frame enlargement)

Bob Hope did a French accent, trying to prove to Claudette Colbert that he had the "goods" that Charles Boyer had. (16mm frame enlargement)

After 3 kisses, which the audience went wild over, Hope said "What a benefit!" (16mm frame enlargement)

Colbert looked at the audience and said "Must be more than just the French accent!" (16mm frame enlargement)

As the music faded, the spotlights came on and Cary Grant, Bob Hope and Claudette Colbert returned to the stage to auction off three fully autographed copies of the Hollywood Victory Souvenir Program. Standing left, right and center, there was a bit of a comedy-drama about which star would get the most money. As the bidding started to climb, Claudette added that she would also give a kiss to the highest bidder. Claudette's sold at $1000.00 while combined, Grant and Hope took in another $750.

Claudette Colbert after a winner's kiss. (16mm frame enlargement)

After intermission, another medley of patriotic songs preceded Frances Langford, who opened the second half with the theme that closed the first half. She sang "Windmill in the Sky," written especially for the Caravan.

Frances Langford bows during her standing ovation. (16mm frame enlargement)

Charles Boyer did his dramatic "The Last Class." He enjoyed an extra round of applause when he came back to the microphone and with his French accent told of becoming an American, and how the whole world depended on the salvation of France and Europe.

Charles Boyer brought out after his act to make his dramatic appeal. (16mm frame enlargement)

Bert Lahr gets instructions from Cary Grant on what is not allowed as a deduction. (16mm frame enlargement)

Bert Lahr turned up as a victim of circumstance playing against Cary Grant in "Pay Your Taxes." Lahr argues that he should get back $49.50 from Uncle Sam, but the tax people did not approve his deduction - Grandma's salary for working as his "gag" man.

Lahr sits amazed at what isn't allowed with the tax collectors. (16mm frame enlargement)

Jerry Colonna was the next act out. After a bit of comedy with Bob Hope, Colonna had a chance to show his talent, doing a trombone solo.

Bob Hope brushes the "dinner crumbs" out of Jerry Colonna's mustache. (16mm frame blow-up)

Colona's preparing his trombone.......(16mm frame blow-up)

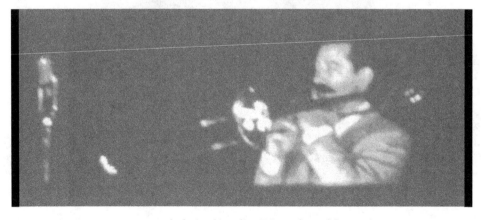

.... and playing his solo. (16mm frame blow-ups)

Then came what was a new Groucho Marx song to the audience. "Dr. Hackenbush", was sung by Groucho with the eight starlets behind him in nurses uniforms and him in a white doctros smock and full make-up. The song is about what a great doctor he is, and was written for the MGM movie "A Day at the Races" but did not survive into the final release.

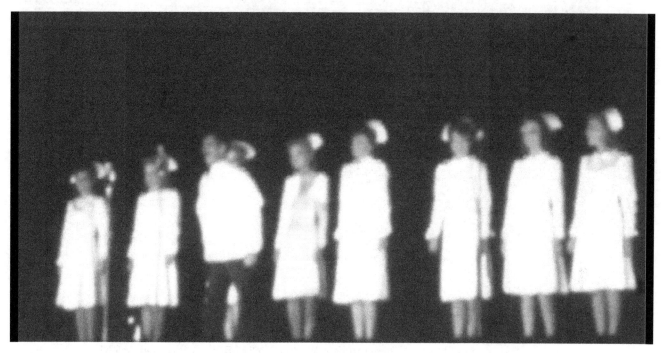

All eight starlets back up Groucho Marx's "Dr. Hackenbush" song. (16mm frame blow-up)

"No matter what I treat them for they die from something else" (16mm frame blow-up)

Cary Grant introduces Merle Oberon to the audience. (16mm frame enlargement)

Merle Oberon, who joined the show to rehearse a full routine, did a reading of "High Flight", written by a young American flyer who was killed serving with the Canadian forces overseas.

Joan Bennett performed in "How to Dismantle an Automobile" with Joan Blondell and Merle Oberon.

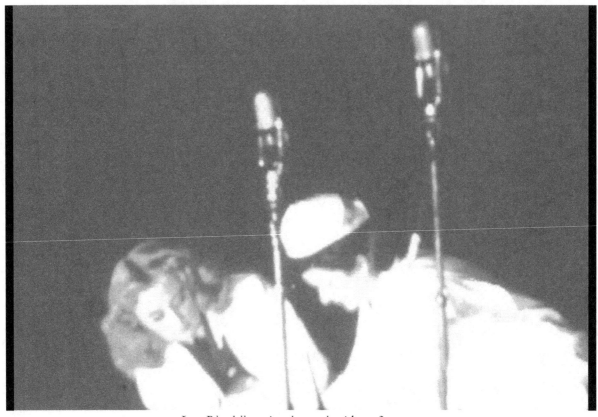

Joan Blondell gets into her mechanic's outfit..........

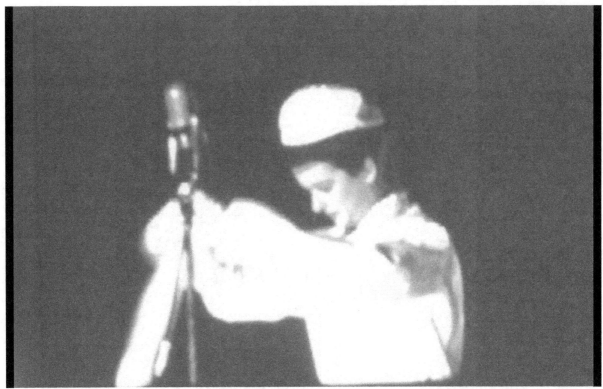

........while Joan Bennett prepares the bandages in "How to Dismantle an Automobile."

Joan Bennett and Merle Oberon take their bows. (16mm frame enlargements)

Rise Stevens, an American operatic singer was the next star up. She sang "My Hero" from "The Chocolate Soldier", an operetta composed in 1908 by Oscar Straus. She also sang a more modern number, "The Moon is Down," based on the John Steinbeck novel of the same name.

Rise Stevens adding a bit of class with her operatically trained voice. (16mm frame enlargement)

The stage went to darkness after her set, and when the light returned, Eleanor Powell was center-stage. She did a full tap dance number, which ended with audience participation. Instructing the audience to keep the beat by clapping their hands against her knees, she had them change to tapping their feet. As this went on, the entire audience picked up speed and were eventually tapping in unison with Powell.

Eleanor Powell tap dancing with the audience. (16mm frame enlargement)

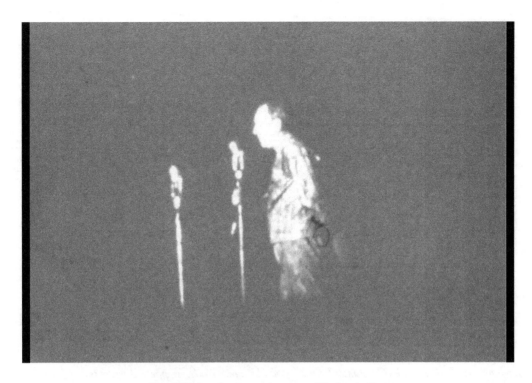

Pat O'Brien demonstrating our soldier's sacrifices.

Pat O'Brien in camouflage comes back to the stage to ask for donations to the Army-Navy relief. (16mm frame enlargements)

        To the music of "We'll Be Back", Pat O'Brien and the sometime comic Frank McHugh held the audience's attention with a portrayal of bravery of the evacuation of Bataan. O'Brien used the drama as an illustration of what the servicemen go through, and with their sacrifices, we need to sacrifice also. Bert Lahr brought along his own "Woodsman Sketch" where he wore a toupee that constantly slipped whenever he chopped at a piece of wood. As he did a spoken-song about the hardships of a woodsman, he was consistently hit with saw dust whenever he opened his mouth wide and did his customary growl, similar to the one he did as "The Cowardly Lion."

Note the odd toupee on Bert Lahr's head. Constantly falling off into his lumber pile, it appeared worse in combing and placement as the skit went on. (16mm frame enlargement)

Jimmy Cagney and the eight starlets came out on stage. Dressed in a Civil War uniform, Cagney did numbers from his yet to be released "Yankee Doodle Dandy." After a rigorous tap dance, backed with flag waving of the eight, Cagney segued into "God Bless America" and "You're a Grand Old Flag." The entire cast joined in the singing and ended the show, around midnight. They went back to the train and by 2 AM, it was on its way to Cleveland.

Jimmy Cagney finishes his number.........

.....and enjoys his standing ovation! (16mm frame enlargements)

Left to right: Ray Middleton (barely visible), Claudette Colbert, Bob Hope, Charles Boyer, Joan Blondell, Bert Lahr, Cary Grant, Eleanor Powell, Oliver Hardy, Stan Laurel, Charlotte Greenwood, Desi Arnaz, Frances Lnngford, and James Cagney. This photo of the finale is from Boston, the city before Philadelphia. Philadelphia ended with a pyrotechnic display in the last act.

CLEVELAND, OHIO - MAY 3, 1942

Hollywood Victory Caravan program - Cleveland, Ohio. Two-color cover with artwork by Gilbert Bundy.

City of Cleveland

FRANK J. LAUSCHE
MAYOR

May 3, 1942

To the Hollywood Victory Caravan:

We are delighted to greet you in the name of the people of Cleveland and of all Northern Ohio who are gathered here today to aid in the great work which the Navy Relief Society and the Army Emergency Relief Society are doing in this time of national effort.

Individually, we have had the pleasure of seeing many of you here in Cleveland before; collectively, you today set a new high standard of unified support of a noble cause. Welcome to Cleveland!

We are proud of the work that Cleveland is doing for the Nation, and we are proud that you have come to our great Public Hall, which has been the auditorium for a number of other events in support of Navy Relief during our "Meet Your Navy Week" that started ten days ago.

Through our Cleveland Advertising Club and the many other clubs which have rallied to its support, we hope that tonight will add generously to the fund which your tour is providing for the Army and Navy Relief funds. We have enjoyed the excitement of preparing for your arrival, and tonight we enjoy your presence.

We shall always remember what you have done for your Country!

Sincerely yours,

Frank J. Lausche

Mayor

FJL:T

Mayor Frank Larriche wrote a letter of thanks. Most of the stars appeared in Cleveland before, including Laurel and Hardy, who had just finished a national theater tour. They appeared in the Palace theater on the week of February 6, 1942.

Mayor Frank Larriche gave full city approval for use of the Public Hall Auditorium for the Hollywood Victory Caravan, which was scheduled for Sunday, May 3rd. Mayor Larriche stated in the days before the show, "This great assembly of stars, whose combined annual income is far in excess of $4,000,000 a year, is unique to the city of Cleveland." Referring to the ticket prices he also said, "It's a bargain bill. We all know that the Navy Relief Society and the Army Emergency Relief Society are doing a wonderful work in bringing immediate aid to the widows and orphans before the slower pension system starts operating to take care of them."

Cleveland went door to door to collect pledges during the week preceding the Caravan.

Patrons and businesses bought everything from single tickets to blocks of tickets and donated them for the servicemen in the area to see the show. Cleveland was in a "Navy Relief Week", and had just had a bond drive parade the previous Thursday to raise money for the war effort. The five largest floats from that parade were saved and parked in various locations downtown. They were used to sell Caravan tickets from. Dorothy Lamour, the actress, worked in one the day that the Caravan train arrived. Other local celebrities joined in to boost ticket sales and ensure a sellout show. Cleveland's top seat price was $10 at the top and $1 at the lowest, with various prices in between. The Warners' theater chain sold tickets in their first run movie houses in the six surrounding cities.

The Statler Hotel, on the corner of Euclid Avenue and 12th Street, donated a full floor for the Caravan for its exclusive use. The trained pulled into the Pennsylvania 55th Street station around 1 PM. Stars were driven directly to the hotel by Cleveland police officers.

The Statler Hotel, corner of Euclid and 12th street in the twenties. Changing little over the years, it now houses 275 appartments, and carries the name "Statler Arms."

In place of actually seeing the stars parade, each theater in Cleveland and the surrounding areas had the newsreel of the Hollywood Victory Caravan arrival and parade from Washington, DC. None of the film, however, contained any of the actual performances.

No events were scheduled for that afternoon, and the Caravan remained at the hotel until that evening's show, with the exception of Groucho Marx. Groucho had left the train at Akron, Ohio, where his brother was appearing in vaudeville. He went into the theater and took a front row seat. In the middle of Chico's act, Groucho started to act up. Not recognized by Chico at first, his brother got up and started to walk out, disturbing everyone in the row. Chico nearly fell off his piano bench when he identified Groucho's voice. Groucho then climbed up on stage and the two famous brothers did an impromptu routine, which brought the house down. He caught a train to Cleveland, and as normal, wasn't recognized by his fellow passengers. A taxi took him to the hotel.

Bert Lahr was a bit upset when he had to wear black shoes with a brown suit. He didn't pack a brown pair.

Chico Marx leading "The Chico Marx Orchestra."

Before the show, the stars did a one hour remote broadcast from the Statler hotel. Each one took their time, and greeted their fans from Detroit over the air. Tom Manning hosted the special hour on WTAM. Manning, who became a good friend of Bob Hope's, was known for years as radio and television's "Dean of the Nations Sportscasters".

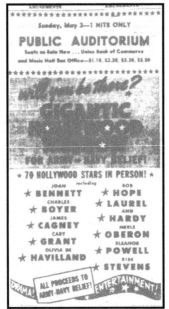

Old newspaper ad for the Cleveland show.

Movie footage was shared by the Hollywood newsreels, which were released quickly for the added advertisement value of seeing your favorite star involved in the show. This snapshot shows the cameramen on their truck's rooftops to get an unobstructed view. The Capitol dome is visible in the background.

The show started on time. Speaking in his opening monologue, Bob Hope told about how the Caravan was doing. He added, "It's the hardest work I've ever had to do in my life and, believe me, I would only do it for nothing."

A local reporter, W. Ward Marsh wrote on May 4th: "Credit for the finished work is due largely to two men. One is producer and director Mark Sandrich and the other is Cleveland's own Bob Hope, who knows how to fill in a gap with or without toothpaste." The toothpaste refers to Hope's radio sponsor Pepsodent toothpaste, closely associated with the star due to his program's consistently high ratings.

The Cleveland audience was very appreciative. Hope said, "I'm so proud of my hometown. I've told my fellow cast members that Cleveland was THE town for quick audience response and hearty appreciation! You never let me down!" Juanita Stark, one of the starlets, was also a Cleveland native.

Total of take? Over 750 tickets were bought and donated back to allow the soldiers free seats. And before Cleveland knew it, three hours of entertainment had passed into history, climaxing more than a week of rallies for Army and Navy Relief.

Response was good, and some reporters commented on how smooth the show went over, considering the rehearsals were done on the train coming from the west coast. The total number of people at the auditorium that Sunday was 10,721. Tickets were from a $10.00 starting rate to a minimum of $1.00. SRO (Standing Room Only) signs had to be placed on the doors a few hours before the show started. Value of the tickets sold came out to $31,667.

Cleveland Public Hall Auditorium, from an old linen postcard.

Cleveland Public Hall Auditorium, interior, looking toward stage. From an old linen postcard.

Detroit, Michigan - MAY 4, 1942

Detroit, Michigan - May 4, 1942.

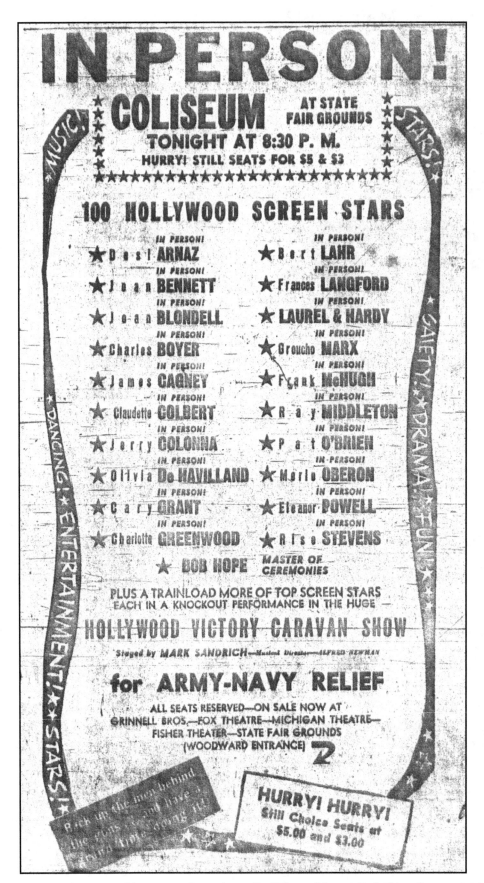

"Back up the men behind the guns and have a grand time doing it"! "Hurry! Hurry! Still Choice Seats at $5.00 and $3.00."

The train itself had been sidetracked in Ohio to permit the stars a must needed rest. It was five hours late, arriving at Detroit's Union Station just after 1 PM. Soldiers from Fort Wayne, Indiana, were assigned to transport the cast to their hotel in olive-drab army staff cars. A 25 man detachment of military police was assigned to keep the overly enthusiastic members of the public from reaching the stars.

The first to disembark was Joan Bennett's black clipped poodle was the first to leave the train. For a half hour, she paraded along the railroad platform on a leash held by Joan Bennett's maid.

Stan Laurel was the first celebrity off the train. Charlotte Greenwood followed, and saw the crowd. Greenwood was never shy and always recognized When she saw a nearby corset factory had people on the roof and filling the windows watching the train, she did a few of her famous high kicks. Normally one of the first ones off, Oliver Hardy slept late, and said he would catch up with everyone at the hotel.

The Statler Hotel continued to provide donated rooms for the Hollywood Victory Caravan. The Detroit Statler Hotel (now demolished) was located at 1539 Washington Boulevard across from Grand Circus Park, in the Foxtown section.

The Hotel Statler as it appeared around 1942, from an old postcard.

Michigan State Fairgrounds Coliseum was chosen as the site of the Caravan show for the May 4th show. The coliseum, built in 1922, is part of the now-defunct Michigan State Fair, which was the oldest state fair in the United States. While modified over the years the building, still in use, appears as it did in the 40's.

The morning of the show, Harry Campbell, vice-president of the Detroit Board of Commerce received a letter from Lieutenant-General H. H. Arnold, the commanding general of the Army Air Forces at Washington requesting a sell-out.:

"I cannot stress sufficiently the importance of the success of this show in your city since it is the opening gun in a campaign to raise money for dependants of soldiers and sailors. I hope that you will assist in the ticket sale by asking all Detroit business men to support the sale of seats and thus insure success."

Local theaters ran the newsreels of the Caravan from Washington, DC and Los Angeles. Detroit's Telenews Theater created new titles for their showing, stating "They're coming to Detroit!", and ran it continuously with their other newsreels until right before the show started.

Detroit's Telenews Theater, built in the early 40's was located on Woodward Avenue.

By 10:00 AM the only tickets remaining were around 600 of the $5.00 seats. By show time, they were sold out. After these sold, they started selling standing room, to the maximum that the fire department would allow, at $2.40 a ticket.

Bob Hope flew to Detroit from Cleveland. Arriving earlier than the train, he had arranged for a benefit game of golf with Mayor Edward Jeffries. Hope left Cleveland Sunday night, right after the show, stating that besides the game, he wanted the early customers their money's worth.

Inviting some of the reporters up to his hotel room, he opened the door in his pajamas and robe with a cheery "Come in and lie down." Appearing tired from lack of sleep and needing a shave, he answered questions for the press. Anticipating a loss in his upcoming 9 holes of golf, Hope quipped, "I'm going to need three caddies today. Two to carry me," he yawned, "and one to carry my bag."

Hope mentioned that the stars "are somewhere near the city. They need the rest, too. This is about the toughest junket you can imagine."

He expressed amazement at the absence of friction between so many stars, who were given alphabetical billing throughout the show. He told the reporters: that there was not "a dime of temperament" between the stars. "Some of these people would walk off the set, even at $150,000 a picture, if they didn't like their dressing rooms. On this trip, they've even dressed in sewers." In one city they had two dressing areas, so they ended up putting the women in one, and the men in the other.

"Why, up in Boston, I dressed in the elephant house. I understand you had a horse show out in your Fair Grounds recently and the odor still lingers. Well, this is the first time I played Fair Grounds since I was a horse."

In addition to his golf game, Hope planned to get together with five of his radio writers, who flew in "from the coast" to prepare the radio show for Hope's broadcast at the Great Lakes Naval Training Station the evening of May 5th.

Bob Hope was not the only one to go "AWOL" that day. Juanita Stark, Jimmy Cagney, Joan Blondell and Pat O'Brien also broke one of their "standing orders". They visited hospitalized children in the Essex County Sanatorium, located in Windsor, Canada, a short drive through the Detroit-Windsor tunnel that connect both countries.

Juanita Stark, Jimmy Cagney, Joan Blondell and Pat O'Brien visiting patients in the Essex County Sanatorium, located in Windsor, Canada.

The Detroit Michigan Fairgrounds Coliseum, as it appeared in 2008, virtually unchanged.

At the coliseum, military police aided in parking the people who will watch the show from seats costing from $1 to $500 dollars. All ticket holders parked for free. Two lots were created near the eastern gate on State Fair Avenue, and near the northern gate on Woodward Avenues. Signs informed patrons where to park, based on which direction they were going when they left. The total attendance that evening was over 5600 people, with proceeds of $53,000.

The interior of the Detroit Michigan Fairgrounds Coliseum, with standing room only.

The Hollywood Victory Caravan started about 45 minutes late due to an electrical problem that evening. The sound had to be reworked. At opening, it was fine until Bob Hope started his monologue. Just into his routine, suddenly half the "sound horns" set up for the evening's show shut down. Just as suddenly they came back up. Hope looked at the audience, and without missing a beat, said: "Ha! We just joined the network!"

Commander D. Dwight Douglas was one of two patrons singled out during the show. During intermission, another autographed copy of the program was auctioned off, this time by Cary Grant and Joan Blondell. Commander Douglas was called to the stage after placing the winning bid of $300. When he went on the stage to receive his book, he was kissed by Joan Blondell. Having about a thousand sailors under his command, with most attending the show that evening, the kiss probably created an exciting day for him when he returned to base.

The second man singled out was an unknown person who decided he had to leave early. When Hope saw him leaving his seat, he became the victim of Bob Hope's verbal wit. The by-play between the both of them brought the house down, with Hope receiving a standing ovation.

Photo of Laurel and Hardy from their latest release "Great Guns" ran in newspapers as publicity for Detroit's Hollywood Victory Caravan Show. Many of the studios provided photographs from the star's latest movies.

The United Detroit Theater felt that the stars were not receiving enough appreciation for their effort. To them the focus was more on the grosses and little on the effort in the weeks after the show. They decided to put together scrapbooks for all the members of the troupe. All the local stories, columns, editorial comments, etc. on the Victory Caravan were gathered from the preceding weeks and put into 50 collections. The scrapbooks were sent to each of the stars, the starlets, directors, writers, and others who contributed to the show.

Stan Laurel's copy of the Hollywood Victory Caravan Scrapbook. Photo courtesy of Lois Laurel-Hawes.

BOB HOPE'S RADIO BROADCAST - MAY 5, 1942

Bob Hope and Frances Langford are greeted.....

....and Jerry Colonna, Frances Langford, and Bob Hope speaking to an unknown military person before doing a broadcast.

There was no performance scheduled for Tuesday, May 5th. The Bob Hope Pepsodent Radio Show was broadcasting live that evening, from the Great Lakes Naval Training Station near Waukegan, Illinois. Bob Hope, along with Claudette Colbert, Francis Langford and Jerry Colonna from the Caravan for the broadcast. The show also featured Skinnay Ennis and Vera Vague, two of his regulars, and Ben Gage as his announcer.

His opening started with him saying: "How ya doing ladies and gentlemen. This is Bob "Priorities" Hope telling you sailors to buy Pepsodent toothpaste and turn in your old tubes [for the war effort] and your teeth will be so bright you can get a new girlfriend and turn in your old tub."

Talking about his trip out, he joked: "You know when a visiting celebrity arrives they always have a big brass band at the station to greet 'em, but for me they had a Campfire girl playing the harmonica!"

Frances Langford came out and sang "Somebody Else Has Taken My Place" to a loud applause from the sailors present. Whenever referring to the Hollywood Victory Caravan's Chicago's performance scheduled for the following evening, Hope constantly brought up the beautiful women on the tour, and then introduced Claudette Colbert for a bit about his cross country trip and his self-acclaimed great looks and personality.

He told the Colbert that he sat between Joan Bennett and Merle Oberon on the train when it left Los Angeles. She expressed disbelief when Hope said he did not attempt to kiss either of them and Hope replied that every time he opened his mouth, smoke came out.

As on the Caravan stage, Hope told Colbert that he was as good looking as any of the leading men on the trip. He said if he had a French accent, he would be as adored by the women as Charles Boyer was. To prove his theory, Hope did the accent, and threw in a few words of French, then kissed Colbert. Colbert feigned impatience and responded, "Must be something more than just his accent" and left the stage to a huge round of cheers and applause from the sailors.

Finishing his radio show at the Great Lakes Naval Training station, he sang a special version of his theme song, "Thanks for the Memories" aimed directly at the sailors in the audience:

> "Thanks for the memories, of you the Navy's pride, we're more than gratified,
> To see your shining faces out there smiling side-by-side, and thank you so much!

> "And thanks for the memories, you Great Lakes boys who train, to free the bounding main,
> You'll live to see the Japanese make their loss our gain, and thank you so much!

> "So folks, join the trend now prevailing, buy bonds and help keep these boys safe,
> This is no time for shirking or failing,
> "Our force to free the seven seas."

He ended the song with "Say, I think I should mention that Claudette Colbert's salary for tonight is going to pay for tickets, for the boys to see the show tomorrow, how 'bout that friends?". This received the biggest roar of the crowd all evening. The response seem to affect Hope so deeply that on his last Caravan mention of the evening, he could only remember seven of the stars by name. A special thanks was made to Rear Admiral John Downes, of the USN for allowing the broadcast from the training station.

Meanwhile, Bing Crosby arrived at the Chicago Hotel Ambassador, finally joining the Caravan.

Bob Hope with Skinnay Ennis at the microphone.

Scheduled for Tuesday evenings, Bob Hope did not miss a broadcast. He was in a seven week tour doing remote broadcasts from different Army and Navy bases. The Hollywood Victory Caravan was added to his busy schedule.

CHICAGO, ILLNOIS - MAY 6, 1942

In Chicago's program there were no photos of the stars, just a double page credit for the show, and information about Army Emergency Relief and Navy Society Relief. The program was given to everyone who attended for free. Printing costs were paid for by Somerset Importers, distributors of Haig & Haig Scots Whisky, and other fine liquors.

COMMANDANT

NINTH NAVAL DISTRICT

GREAT LAKES, ILLINOIS

April 29, 1942

Dear Ladies and Gentlemen:

The officers and men of the United States Navy, Marines, and Coast Guard, extend a heart-felt "Thank you" to the ever generous citizens of Chicago for their magnificent support of this "Hollywood Victory Caravan".

The enthusiastic cooperation of these motion picture actors and actresses, and the untiring work of the citizens whose efforts have made this show possible will be gratefully remembered by the Navy Relief Society.

To everyone whose support has made this show a success, may I extend the assurance that you are making a direct contribution to our war effort. You are enabling the Army and the Navy Relief Societies to carry forward their vitally important work of protecting and caring for the loved ones of our fighting men.

We extend our best wishes for a most enjoyable evening.

Sincerely yours,

JOHN DOWNES,
Rear Admiral, U.S. Navy.

Letter of thanks to the citizens of Chicago, from The Ninth Naval District.........

WAR DEPARTMENT
HEADQUARTERS SIXTH CORPS AREA
UNITED STATES POST OFFICE BUILDING
CHICAGO, ILLINOIS

THE COMMANDING GENERAL.

May 6, 1942.

The Guests of The Hollywood Victory Caravan
Chicago Stadium
Chicago, Illinois.

Dear Guests:

On behalf of Army Emergency Relief, I would like to express our deep gratitude and appreciation to the many thousands of patriotic guests and our distinguished entertainers who are doing so much to help carry on the work at home for those in our armed forces who are carrying the fight to the enemy.

Your presence tonight not only indicates your patriotism but your desire to see that the loved ones of your soldiers and sailors shall suffer no privations.

Our enjoyment of this outstanding program should be enhanced by the knowledge that the funds derived will go to meet emergencies in the families of those uppermost in our thoughts at this critical time.

You are advised that Army Emergency Relief cooperates with and is supplemental to the Red Cross which by Law is the basic source of assistance to the armed forces. Army Emergency Relief, by mutual agreement with the Red Cross, takes care of emergency cases restricted to Army jurisdiction under which the Red Cross is limited in its function.

Again, I thank all of you.

Sincerely yours,

GEORGE GRUNERT
Major General, U. S. Army
Commanding

....and the Headquarters of Army Sixth Corp Area.

The train left Detroit shortly before 2 am, and was planned to sidetrack for a few hours on the way, again affording the stars some rest. People woke up the morning of May 5th to read the following headline: "TRAIN ACCIDENT DELAYS STARS ON ROUTE TO CHICAGO FOR HOLLYWOOD VICTORY CARAVAN PERFORMANCE."

The 11 car Hollywood Victory Caravan left Detroit after 1 AM after finishing the three-and-one-half hour show at the Michigan State Fair Coliseum. The train was guarded by the Army and Navy personnel that were provided by the government , as any major war weapon would be. On this trip, very few stars remained. Most elected to go on to the hotel earlier to get the rest they were missing. Although the train was very opulent, and had its own restaurant chefs, most of the stars wanted the relaxation and dining excellence that the Hotel Ambassador with its famous Pump Room restaurant could provide. They were looking forward to a day of rest.

The Caravan train had been sidetracked in Ohio to allow the stars remaining some time to rest. When it started off again, it struck a car at a grade crossing near Monroe, Michigan, south of Detroit. The car was demolished, but the female driver was spared injury. Although all grade crossings (level street crossings) were cleared by soldier prior to the train going through, the woman occupying the vehicle had ignored the signals and became stuck on the tracks.

The train had slowed down, and after a try at restarting the vehicle, the driver and soldiers were cleared from the immediate area. Unable to come to a full stop in time, it struck the front of the car, causing the car to be totaled. The train, however, was not damaged beyond a few scratches. The investigation lasted a few hours and the train was allowed to continue to Chicago. Neither the woman or the train engineer were ticketed or arrested.

Stan Laurel is to the right, and Desi Arnaz on the left of three of the Hollywood Victory Caravan's starlets, some of the few stars left on the train.

After their arrival in Chicago, according to Walter Winchell, Bert Lahr went up to the first policeman he encountered. Knowing he would not be recognized, he told the policeman that he was travelling with the Hollywood Victory Caravan show. "In Boston," he said, "I had a lot of good luck picking pockets. I was wondering if you had any objections to me trying my luck here in Chicago? Every pocket I pick I will keep you in mind!" According to Winchell, the cop "thought it would be all right!" Lucky for the officer, neither Winchell or Lahr knew the officer's name.

Wolfe Kaufman, a local columnist, had time to meet the stars at the hotel before they headed to the Chicago Coliseum. Commenting on the old (prewar) movie formula of "boy meets girl", Wolfe had stated the need for a change. Due to the fact that most of the boys were fighting, the only alternative left was to use "man meets girl" instead.

While prewar show business was always a "business of youth," all that remained in Hollywood today were exemplified by the cast of the Hollywood Victory Caravan. While the "girls" were young, the male stars were made up of Bob Hope, Bing Crosby, Charles Boyer, Cary Grant, Jimmy Cagney, Laurel and Hardy and more from the same age group.

Bob Hope and Bert Lahr were seen to blush when age was mentioned and quickly changed the subject. Crosby, Grant and Cagney were the babies of the group among the male celebrities. They're all 38 years old. O'Brien and Boyer admitted to 43 each. Groucho claimed to be 47 (actually 51). Stan Laurel and Oliver Hardy said they were 50 (Laurel was soon to be 52).

The pictures are changing reported Kaufman, but far from poking fun at the grey-at-the-temples generation, he felt it was a pleasure that they still were carrying on, doing their bit for the war effort. In comparison, most of the female stars were still in their early 20's

Bing Crosby, who just joined the troupe the evening before, was asked about his compensation. He replied, "Compensation! Are you kidding? What greater compensation can there be for a four time papa like me than to know I'm helping where it counts...!"

Earlier that day Crosby and Hope played in their first Professional Golfers' Association (PGA) sponsored a war relief golf tour. Proceeds from this game went to Fort Sheridan Athletic Fund. Crosby and Chick Evans beat Hope and Tony Amour by 2 strokes. Hope and Crosby both took their golf seriously. Hope challenged Crosby to a personal five- match series. Starting with this game, Crosby was now one game ahead. For nine holes, Crosby and Evans shot even par 36s. Amour shot 37 and Hope came in last with a 38 score.

Old newspaper photo of (left to right) Tommy Armour, Chick Evans, Bing Crosby and Bob Hope.

The match had to be stopped after nine holes, because of the movement of the crowds. According to the manager and director of the tour, Fred Corcocan the crowd was around 5000 people. The end total was estimated at a minimum of $2500. This figure included the service men who were not charged admission.

Hope and Crosby returned to the hotel to prepare for the Caravan show . Crosby did not broadcast his radio show on May 7, or 14. His replacement for both programs was his son, Bob Crosby.

Chicago Stadium at night, from an old linen postcard.

Original six column newspaper ad

The Chicago Stadium was packed by 19,823 people, and took in $87,761. Officials noted that it was unlikely that any of the remaining cities would equal this huge amount. The total was increased to $90,000 with a concessioner's additional donation.

Chicago's program opened with Rear Admiral John Downes and Major General George Grunert reading greetings from Secretary of the Navy Knox and Secretary of War Henry L. Stimson. Called up to the stage was Mayor and Mrs. Edward J. Kelly of Chicago and Governor of Illinois Dwight Herbert Green and his wife. When they left the stage, the Star Spangled Banner started, and the evening from that point on belonged to the audience.

The show preceded as usual, with an orchestra of forty. This night had the addition of Bing Crosby. With his songs added the show ran over 4 hours, finishing thirty-five minutes past midnight.

Cary Grant and Bob Hope shared the masters of ceremonies position. When introduced to the audience they always did a bit of "patter" together. Typical of the style of humor, Hope told Grant that getting around during wartime was rough. "I've got seniority on by priority, but I have to wait until I get the authority of the majority to get the authority of the Authorities" he said, which during the time of rationing boards brought down the house.

When Hope and Crosby were on the stage together, beside their normal "barbs", they did a routine of two Chicago politicians trying to pick each other's pockets. At one point Hope was so flustered with the ad-libbing, he looked into the audience and said, "Talk amongst yourselves for a bit. I'll remember my lines!"

Jimmy Cagney remembers Chicago as the first city he saw Bing Crosby work. For the song "Blues of the Night" Crosby wore orange flannels, and a blue slope coat with brass zoot buttons, one of the styles of the day. Cagney thought that his choices of colors proved the rumor that Crosby was color-blind. Cagney also remembered that when Bob Hope said "well, I'm sure you're all ready to hear the Groaner......." the audience exploded as Crosby came in. After saying "wadda yez want to hear?" the audience exploded again. Turning to the orchestra leader Al Newman, he shouted "Hit it now!" He encored with a few more songs.

Cagney said "when Bing came off stage, the perspiration on him was a revelation to me. Here he had been to all appearances perfectly loose and relaxed, but not at all. He was giving everything he had in every note he sang."

According to Jimmy Cagney, Groucho Marx, preparing for a career beyond the Marx Brothers did his "Where's Olive?" sketch with de Havilland for the first time without his greasepaint eyebrows or mustache. When the newspaper photo on the following day identified him as Groucho when he performed "Dr. Hackenbush" in full makeup and as Harpo when he performed without, he had second thoughts about what he had done.

Charles Boyer, who had recently become a citizen, announced to the audience that he was "the youngest American" in the stadium. He then proceeded to bring tears to the audience by explaining why he "abandoned his lovely France." Boyer ended with, "France may be captive, but the French race will live - side-by-side with you, with us Americans." This was the one of the only somber points of the evening, although most of the acts underlined the import of America's struggle of the day.

At intermission, Cary Grant, Bob Hope, Merle Oberon and Claudette Colbert came out on stage, and auctioned off signed programs. High bidder Morris B. Sachs, sponsor of Chicago's Amateur Hour bought the first one at $1000. In return, besides the program, Sachs received a kiss from Claudette Colbert. Sachs then sold the same program to another bidder, Mrs. Ethel Hoffa. For the additional $500 donation, she pulled back the veil of her hat, and received a thank you kiss from Cary Grant and Bob Hope. That was a total of $1500 made on the first program alone! The audience yelled loudly.

Caught up in the excitement, Bob Hope took the mike again and shouted "We want at least $500 dollars for the next one. If it doesn't reach at least that, the winner this time will get to kiss Charlotte Greenwood!"

Francis Pope, from the $3.00 balcony seats won the next one for $600. Taking a short while to reach the stage, Hope watched him clime up and could not resist saying "What's the dope, Pope!" After the kiss from Colbert,

Pope shouted "It was worth it!" Two men who represented a root beer company bought the third program for $700 bringing the intermission total up to $2800.

Directly after the show there was a quick backstage reception with the stars for the special $50-a-seat guests of honor. Due to the extended length of the show, there were only time for a few quick hellos and good-byes. The Hollywood Victory Caravan had to hurry back to the Hotel Ambassador, pack, and get back to the train. Their next show was in St. Louis.

Morris B. Sachs Amateur Hour, sponsored by Sachs Department Store was a staple on radio (WENR) and television (WENR-TV). A Chicago businessman and philanthropist, he was the high bid of $1000 on one of the auctioned Hollywood Victory Caravan autographed programs His show was one of the highest rated local shows in Chicago, sadly no copies of either exist today. Some of the people who owe their careers to this program were singers Frankie Laine and Mel Torme, as well as actress Pamela Britten.

Rare photo of Mrs. Ethel Haffa holding her autographed program while getting her kiss from Cary Grant while Morris B. Sachs looks on.

Laurel and Hardy doing their Driver's License routine on stage. Army officials were seated to the left and Navy officials to the right, behind their respective symbols.

"'Harpo' Marx, Olivia de Haviland, and Jerry Colonna look over the script." Even with his hat pulled down and the book held up, Groucho and his brothers look so much alike that without make-up Groucho was hard to identify.

ST LOUIS, MISSOURI - May 7, 1942

  In 1941 the USO was chartered by the United States congress as a non-profit civilian agency and the First Saint Louis USO was opened at the Municipal Auditorium July 19, 1941. Other USO centers were opened throughout the country to support the service men and women during WWII and beyond. On May 7, 1942, The Hollywood

Victory Caravan was scheduled to play here. A unique feature of the auditorium was that it was split into two; the front of the building was the Opera House. It was possible to use both sides at once as the stages were back to back.

Old linen postcard, from the early 40's.

Standing Room Only as 12,369 people fill an auditorium build for less than 10,000.

The train arrived early in the morning. Announced to be in at 1 PM at Union Station, the train pulled in several hours before, however without the outside banner and the heavy curtains drawn shut, it drew no immediate attention. Around noon, Bing Crosby stepped off the train onto the platform to stretch. He was not recognized and no one paid any attention.

Bob Hope was up around the same time. Going for the diner car to get lunch, he spotted a pile of newspapers set aside for the stars. Grabbing the papers, he went up and down the train with shouts of "Get today's news here. Fresh news!" He explained to whoever asked that he was "going to make something on this trip after all!"

Mayor William Dee Becker had declared this Thursday as "Army and Navy Relief Day." He was on route to train station set to greet the stars personally that morning. Reporters and several hundred spectators were on the platform. The first one of the stars to step onto the platform was Bing Crosby. Informed by the other members of the reception committee that the Mayor still had not arrived, Crosby asked what party he was. Republican was the reply. "Well, we better wait for him, then," Crosby retorted. "There are only a couple of them left." (FDR was a Democrat, and so was most of his administration.)

Hope joined Crosby on the platform, the Mayor arrived and gave greetings. Hope and Crosby hurried off the stage, and by-passing the parade cars, which were waiting, the sought their own transportation. They had a second golf game to play, this time at Meadow Brook Country Club against two local players, so left on their own.

Cary Grant received a rousing reception, accented with feminine screams. Mentioning he worked with the Metropolitan Opera years ago under his real name, Archibald Leach. He inquired of its plans for the season before he moved on.

Olivia de Havilland exited and was greeted. She was carrying three books. One was a volume of Roosevelt's speeches, while the second one was of Chekhov's short stories. She never responded to the reporter's questions of what the third one was. Adding to the interest, she claimed she was using the fly leaves of the third book to write a letter to Henry Luce, publisher of Life magazine. It seems she was protesting an article that appeared about her.

Laurel and Hardy accepted the Mayor's greeting, and when they saw the crowd, they went right into a bit. Hardy accepted the thanks while Laurel kept trying to interrupt him. Finally when Ollie acknowledges Stan, he finds out he was standing on Stan's foot during his entire acceptance speech

Groucho was not recognized by many when he stepped off the train out of his "character" make-up.

Reporters lined the route to the cars, each trying to get a statement they could call exclusive. Various members of the troupe said the comic relief on the train was mostly provided by Pat O'Brien and Bert Lahr. Pat O'Brien gave another credit in "The Wind At My Back," his autobiography. He said "*With all the greatest stars on hand, the greatest ovation and reception all across the country were always to Laurel and Hardy. Every time they made their entrance, there were loud bursts of applause and cheers.*"

Groucho was praised for the after dinner community sing-a-longs on the train, helping to keep morale high. One by one the stars came out and heading to the waiting cars. The last out were Claudette Colbert, and the 8 starlets. Seventy soldiers and 70 soldiers accompanied the stars throughout their St. Louis visit.

From the station to the Hotel Jefferson, the downtown crowd was estimated between 50,000 to 70,000. Street cars were stopped along the route and people climbed onto the sides of these stalled cars to get a better view.

Office workers hung out of their windows to spot the stars. In spots, the parade had to be stopped as the crowd was pushed back.

Original 1942 postcard of the Hotel Statler in St. Louis.

Hope and Crosby disappointed the crowd by not appearing in the parade. Constant cries of "Where's Hope" followed the entire parade. About half the stars left when the parade arrived at the Hotel Statler. Staying at this hotel were Claudette Colbert, Merle Oberon, Frances Langford, Joan Blondell, Cary Grant, Ray Middleton, Desi Arnaz, Jimmy Cagney, Jerry Colonna and Pat O'Brien.

The Jefferson Hotel, from an old linen postcard.

The remainder of the party went to the Hotel Jefferson, which, like the Hotel Statler, donated the stay for the Caravan. Slow traffic and multiple starts and stops as the crowd tightened made this trip slower than the first part.

Laurel and Hardy got off at the Twelfth Boulevard entrance to the hotel and were immediately mobbed. It took quite a few soldiers and sailors to clear a path to the door. The police were busy at the hotel's Locust Street entrance, clearing a path for the rest of the entourage.

The stars who stayed at the Hotel Jefferson were Joan Bennett, Olivia de Havilland, Stan Laurel, Oliver Hardy, Rise Stevens, Eleanor Powell, Charlotte Greenwood, Bob Hope, Bing Crosby, Charles Boyer, Bert Lahr, Groucho Marx, and Frank McHugh.

Bob Hope and Bing Crosby finally made it to the Meadow Brook Country Club. The game started at 2:30 in the afternoon due to autograph requests before Crosby and Hope reached their vehicle. The requests did not stop when they arrived at the course. An announcement had to be made over the loudspeakers that no more signatures would be given. Since the Caravan show was scheduled for 8:30 that evening, play had to start to get the stars back in time to prepare. The crowd was filled with 2000 spectators, all happy to pay the $1 admission fee.

When they reached the first tee, Crosby joined with Bob Morse (trick shot artist) and Hope paired with Johnny Manion (Meadow Brook's club pro). It was hard to keep the onlookers away from the tee and off the fairway, until Crosby topped his first shot and the ball bounced into the crowd. After this, the spectators showed considerably more respect. Hope tried to pitch across a creek and under some tree branches at hole 3. The ball hit a small five year old girl. She stated that she was not hurt, but persons around her could see a lump on her head.

Hope was extremely annoyed at the people in the crowd and suggested they cease play. Crosby spoke to the crowd, pointing out the danger of injury if a ball hits a person. The crowd stayed back on hole 4, but by hole 5 they fringed the fairway again. The game had to finally be called, after 12 holes, due to the uncontrollable crowd and the time it took to play each hole. The game still counted on the Hope-Crosby bet, however, and Crosby was now ahead by 2 games.

Each ad was different in star order and inclusion in the St. Louis newspaper ads. For example, this ad is missing Bing Crosby, who oddly enough was on the list in many towns he never played. Note the order of billing changed away from alphabetical.

After the parade, Cary Grant went to the American Theater, to watch rehearsals by the Municipal Opera chorus. From there, he was driven over to Forest Park to revisit the theater there. Red Cross Motor Corp drivers were assigned to drive the stars. Miss Virginia Hinton Lewis offered to drive him wherever he wanted to go, but was turned down. Grant chose a convertible over her car. When she heard that he was choosing a different vehicle, she offered to "chop the top" off her car, just to have the honor of being Grant's chauffer. The convertible was owned by Mrs. Robert Larimore. After a bit of discussion, Grant said that they should all go. Mrs. Larimore ended up driving.

The auditorium opened at 7:30 and started filling. In St. Louis tickets ranged from $1.10 for standing room to $11.for choice seats, with most seats under $5. By Thursday morning all seats were sold out, and only standing room was left. There were sixteen boxes seating six patrons each that were bought by the Mayor, his party, and local companies. Total ticket sales were 12,369 bringing in $41,000.

When Bob Hope came out on stage that evening, he had a bit of trouble being heard. The audience expressed dissatisfaction, and, as in Boston, the shouting consisted of "louder, Hope" and "can't hear you, Bob!" When Hope finally reached the level needed, another voice was heard to shout " louder, and funnier!"

Again, as in Boston, hand microphones had to be used throughout the show. Notes were also referred to by some of the stars, to ensure they did not miss any lines. Anytime something happened backstage, Bob Hope would let the audience know what was happening. A few of the acts were switched in order this time for various technical problems.

Desi Arnaz started the evening. Groucho Marx's "Where's Olive?" was next, performed with Olivia de Havilland. Marx left his mustache off for this evening's performance, and to help would recognize him, he ad-libbed quite a bit. The sketch, originally written by John and Mary Thorndyke, was focused on a discussion about the wish of the daughter to buy a pair of alligator shoes. As the skit progressed, Groucho thought the alligator would be better off without shoes.

When Cary Grant was introduced, Hope referred to Grant's dimples. This started the crowd laughing. Grant, not hearing his intro, asked the audience several times "What is happening?" This brought more laughter, each time he said it. As everyone settled down, Grant continued the show. Talking to the audience about when he worked in St. Louis, he told the audience that his name was not what Hope introduced. Re-introducing himself as "Archie Leach", the audience became wildly appreciative, especially those who remembered seeing him on stage during those years.

When Jerry Colonna finished his portion that evening, he ended by thanking the audience in a way that was appreciated by the audience. "After the show," he said, "I want you all to come backstage! I want all your autographs!"

Even with the sound issues, and all the interplay between the audience and the performers, the show still finished on time.

"With Beat Wishes From Jerry Colonna."

ST PAUL/MINNEAPOLIS, MINNESOTA - May 8, 1942 - Arrival

Stan Laurel's "official scroll from the King of Saint Paul's Winter Carnival, making them honorary citizens of the "Rollicking Realm of King Boreas VIII." (Photo courtesy of Lois Laurel-Hawes, Stan Laurel's Daughter.)

Stan Laurel, Oliver Hardy, Cary Grant and Desi Arnaz working through the crowd at St. Paul's Union Station.

There were no performances scheduled for Friday, May 8th, allowing the stars a short time off to relax and to prepare for Saturday's two shows. Nearly 5000 fans filled the station platforms when the Caravan Special arrived at St. Paul's Union Station the morning of May 8th. The first people off the train included Oliver Hardy, Stan Laurel, Alma Carol, and Charlotte Greenwood.

A six foot high wooden platform had been erected at the south end of the concourse and a drum-and-bugle corps played as the train pulled in. Nearly 200 drum majorettes were lined up in a double row from the platform to the "stage." Coordinated, each majorette saluted as the stars passed her place in line.

When all the stars were gathered, Mark Sandrich went up to the microphone and thanked the gathered city officials, calling this "the most heartwarming reception we have had in any city." He then introduced each star individually, and each one ascended the stage, took a bow, and received a "Royal Scroll" from the King and Queen of Saint Paul's Winter Carnival, making them honorary citizens of the "Rollicking Realm of King Boreas VIII."

Joan Blondell at Union Station in St. Paul.

Laurel and Hardy came to the platform, and instead of talking to the crowd, they did some "in character" waiving, not interrupting the shouts and applause of the onlookers. Eleanor followed behind the team, having nothing other to say than she "spoke best" with her feet.

Bob Hope was not at the station, however. He had extended their stay in St. Paul to get some much needed rest. On the 9th, he flew in to start their Victory Caravan fundraiser PGA game very early in the morning. He joined Bing Crosby at Midland Hills Country Club. Crosby played with golf pro Wally Mund while Hope partnered with Harry Cooper. Hope-Cooper won the game one up. They had only scheduled 12 holes due to the need to be back in time for the matinee show starting at 2:30 in St. Paul. With the 8:30 show in Minneapolis that evening, it put the team in front of an audience for almost 15 hours that day.

Bing Crosby, left, golf pro Wally Mund, golf superstar "Lighthorse" Harry Cooper and Bob Hope play in a war relief exhibition at Midland Hills near St. Paul.

All the stars present were greeted by St. Paul's Mayor John J. McDonough, and Minneapolis' Mayor Marvin L. Kline. William J. Hickey was the chairman of the reception committee, and Clarence A. Maley, president of the Winter Carnival association, who sponsored the show. Also on the welcoming team for the Army Releif were General Ellard A. Walsh, and Colonel Harry J. Keely, commander of Fort Snelling. Representing the Navy Committee was Commander Joseph Baer.

The stars, having gone through their public reception in St. Paul, returned to the train. The train went directly to Minneapolis' Milwaukee Station where they went through another short ceremony, this one of waving crowds as they left the train, and taken to the busses ready to go to the Hotel Nicolet. There were a line-up of navy men from Word-Chamberlain Field and army men from Fort Snelling were on both sides of the street leading from the Milwaukee station to the hotel in order to hold the crowds back. The stars waved at the thousands of people gathered on the way to the hotel.

An 8:00 press conference had been announced to the reporters. Apparently the stars were not aware of it. Since it was officially declared an evening off, there were no personalities to be seen. Connie Krebs, representative of RKO pictures and Andy Kelly of the Hays office greeted the reporters as they arrived. Together Krebs and Kelly tried to find a few stars for the interviewers.

The reception for the Hollywood Victory Caravan in Milwaukee Station.

Reporters went out on their own, to a few well known eateries in Minneapolis to see who might have stayed local. Some reporters wound up finding Bing Crosby, Groucho Marx (who was not immediately recognized), Desi Arnaz and several of the starlets sitting at a large table together. Crosby apologized for not being at the hotel and said "Come back of the stage at the matinee and we'll talk a lot. I can tell you a lot."

The Nicollet Hotel was in the block surrounded by Washington, Nicollet, Hennepin, and Third Street, Minneapolis. From an old postcard.

"Where's Bob Hope?" the writer queried? Crosby stated he did not know for sure, but he had heard that Hope arrived just a short while ago by plane.

Crosby introduced Groucho. Reporters noticed how much he looked like his brothers without make-up. One of the questions asked of him was "Where's Harpo?" Whatever Groucho answered is unknown, and was said to have been unprintable.

The reporter Jules L. Steele went back to the hotel to see if any stars came in. He saw Andy Kelly of the Hays office who said: "I have Rise Stevens on the telephone. She's gone to bed. Want to talk to her?" Steele enjoyed the conversation, and thought he and Rise would have become good friends if they ever met face to face. The reporter expressed his disappointment with the movie "The Chocolate Soldier" that she starred in with Nelson Eddy. Although she never said it directly, the reporter felt that she shared his opinion. She politely excused herself and the interviews for that evening were finished.

Leaving Milwaukee Station in Minneapolis, Minnesota, as photographed by a fan. Visible on the train are Cary Grant, Charlotte Greenwood, Jimmy Cagney and Charles Boyer, among others.

ST PAUL/MINNEAPOLIS, MINNESOTA - May 9, 1942

Autographed program signed for the highest bidder during an intermission.

The St. Paul show began sharply at 2:30 in the St. Paul Municipal Auditorium and stayed just under its 3 1/2 hour performance time. Alfred Newman, the musical director, was described as being a bundle of nervous energy while he conducted the orchestra. Never really noticed by the audience, it was Newman that the stars focused on for their musical accompaniment and cues. In each performance he faced a new orchestra made up of his traveling 14 and with the addition of 24-30 local musicians. In 1942 he was the musical director for Twentieth Century Fox.

Great notices were given to the overall quality of the show. Besides Newman, Mark Sandrich received praise for his producing of the entire affair. All were amazed at the little amount of time that it took to whip together this project, knowing that it took only a fraction of the time needed to put together a full Hollywood movie. Formerly with RKO, Sandrich was at that time connected to Paramount studios. He was spotted a few times in the audience, listening to the quality of the sound from the stage. All went well that night.

Singled out was Bob Hope's announcing, as well as Cary Grant and Pat O'Brien, who by then was introducing the non-comic performances, such as Charles Boyer and Merle Oberon's.

In a 1972 interview, Bob Hope recalled some of the simple gags that he put over on the Caravan stage, and he was amazed at how well they went over. On introducing Cary Grant, he mentioned that he and Grant had a quick bit. Hope told the audience that he would play the president of Pepsi Cola and Grant the president of Coca-Cola, meeting on the street. Both walked out toward each other, hands extended for a handshake. Hope said "Hello." Grant said "Hello". Then they both belched.

While ad-libbing with Grant, Hope asked about Grant's jacket. Grant answered that his jacket was made of Scotch heather. Hope did not know what his jacket was made from. With great timing one of the orchestra leapt to his feet and shouted, "It's made of Mississippi seaweed."

Bob Hope had some facial scars that he acquired when he was working as a young boy as a tree cutter's assistant. His job was to tie rope to trees that were cut to remove, so the tree's fall could be controlled. One afternoon he had been working on a tree that was cut more than it should have been. As he leaned against the tree to tie the rope, the tree came down, and he went down with it, branches cutting into his face. When asked, Hope always felt that his whole profile, including his famous nose, were created by this accident.

Claudette Colbert came out on stage that evening and asked Bob Hope "Is it true that you got those scars wrestling an alligator?" His response was "Naw, I got them reaching for a second lump of sugar in a St. Paul restaurant." This was a remark the audience could connect with, due to the sugar shortages going on at the time.

St. Paul Auditorium, from an old linen postcard.

When Jerry Colona came out, Hope introduced the two of them as farmers meeting on the street. Colonna interlocked his fingers, palms facing Hope and thumbs down, and started walking toward Hope. They each said hello as Hope reached out and started "milking" Colonna's thumbs.

The only real problem of the evening was Merle Oberon's. When leaving for the show from the Hotel Nicolet that day, she left her stage outfit back in her room. A police car was sent out, with sirens blaring, to pick up the dress. It arrived in time for Oberon' to perform that night. The audience was never aware of the "glitch."

Over 10,000 spectators saw the show, which grossed $28,329.00, exceeding everyone's expectations. Local reporters referred to it as an "overpowering generous performance." No complaints from the audience either, rather a recurring effort of standing ovations were given throughout the show.

The trip from the St. Paul Auditorium to the Nicolet Hotel went smoothly. With just a few minutes of arriving and freshening up, the stars came down to the Hotel Nicolet lobby for a makeshift press conference. The ever impatient reporters, knowing that they were not so lucky the day prior, just traveled through the hotel, making their own luck. Some stars, like Cary Grant, allowed reporters into his room, while others like Joan Blondell and Claudette Colbert posed on the stairs.

St. Paul resident Leo Lynn went into the hotel with a letter of introduction from her cousin, Rise Stevens. Lynn had worked at Paramount as Crosby's stand-in. The letter allowed her through the police cordon and into the hotel, where Crosby not only welcomed her with open arms, he also introduced her to Frank McHugh and Jimmy Cagney who were in his room. "He's a regular fellow" she told the reporters. Interviews were short since the stars were scheduled to start their second show that evening at 8:30. The show went on without any problems and was seen by 9,503 patrons for a total of $33,750.

Minneapolis Auditorium.

DES MOINES, IOWA - May 10, 1942

Des Moines was the only city to totally sell out before the day of the show. Good advertising and promotion made this somewhat smaller stop a great addition to the Army-Navy Relief coffers. Running an ad in the days before the show, for tickets not claimed created such a rush at the box office that all 167 tickets sold out within 4 hours of the box office opening. The total ticket sales for Des Moines came to 4300 with a total of $22,474 in box office receipts.

The ad that sparked the sell-out!

The train arrived at the Rock Island Station at 8:00 in the morning of May 10th. Stars started getting up around 11 AM, and started to leave the train in time for the first actual full parade since Boston. Stars were brought to the State Capitol to start the parade from the capitol to the Shrine Auditorium. Originally scheduled to end at 14th Street, the parade was extended to 18th Street. Due to the fact that the tickets sold out so early, and the auditorium sat just over 4,000 it was decided to give everyone in town a look at the stars with a parade. By the estimate of Joe Loehr, Chief of Police, this parade was viewed by over 200,000. H. A. Alber, Assistant Chief of Police rode in the front of the parade and was reported saying: "I rode ahead of the parade the entire distance and didn't see an unoccupied spot anywhere. Only the parade for President Roosevelt had a similar crowd, but the parade route was considerably longer."

Radio station WHO never stopped announcing the show, and bought a block of tickets totaling $1,633.50 using the proceeds of the station's Golden Glove boxing tournaments. Station WHO donated them to the Iowa American Legion. The American Legion selected 99 mothers of soldiers, one for each county, to attend and represent all the Gold Star and Blue Star mothers at this Mother's Day performance. These mothers were presented with roses by the Des Moines Florist Association, and met at the Banker's Life Auditorium, from there marching to the Shrine Auditorium.

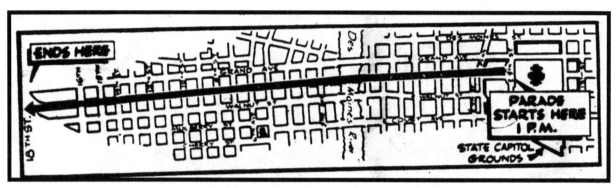

The parade route, from the State Capitol to the Shrine Auditorium down Locust Street to 18th Street, almost 2 miles long.

Most of the stars rode in convertibles, one to a car. Laurel and Hardy shared a miniature automobile, sitting on the back of the open-topped car. Groucho Marx was in full costume and make-up, having taken a position on a ladder of a fire truck. Marx had become an Honorary Member of the Des Moines Fire Department. Three hundred state guardsmen, 500 boy scouts, soldiers, sailors and police officers joined in keeping the parade route open. The parade included several local bands, and the West Des Moines Drum and Bugle Corps.

Stan Laurel and Oliver Hardy ride their parade car and wave to the crowd. Photo from a snapshot taken by a parade spectator. With the balance of weight, Laurel and Hardy were almost tossed into the street as it curved into a driveway and bumped up the approach.

The red, white and blue collection banner.

Laurel and Hardy in an old newspaper clipping.

Streets were decorated with flags, bunting and welcome streamers. Confetti was thrown from downtown buildings as the stars passed. A red, white and blue banner for the Army-Navy Relief funds was carried by military personnel in the front portion of the parade. Spectators were encouraged by loudspeakers to toss coins and bills into it. E.F. Fitzgerald, a guard at the local Iowa-Des Moines bank, and Sam Horowitz kept up a lively patter, and had to empty the banner at least five times into the car behind Frank McHugh. When the donations became unwieldy, and the banner became hard to empty, sailors on either side held out their hats to collect the funds.

Counting from the parade took place in the safe of the Iowa-Des Moines bank. The total amount collected was 14,551 pennies, 10,221 nickels, 9604 dimes, 4624 quarters, 1121 half dollar pieces, and a bale of one and five dollar bills. Also in the banner was 40c Canadian, a roll of dimes and a marble, among other items. The counting took over 3 hours, and the total amount added another $3428 to the total.

The exterior of Shrine Auditorium, Des Moines, Iowa.

All attendees of the parade that did not have tickets for the show were welcome to attend a concert at Fort Des Moines army post induction center. Lieutenant Cornel V. L. Padgett announced that the band would play between 3 to 6 PM. While it rained most of the day, it stayed dry during the entire parade.

Because the crowds slowed the parade the show did not start on time. A buffet lunch with soft drinks was set up for the performers, and reporters were allowed backstage for interviews.

The interior of Shrine Auditorium, Des Moines, Iowa, just prior to the performance.

Joan Blondell lounged on a "prop bed" most of the time when not on stage. Jimmy Cagney was noticed talking to a few stage hands, talking about old times when he was "on the road".

Cary Grant was gracious with everyone he met. He responded to reports that the people living on the west coast were nervous with the war in one word: "Rot!" "Hell, no," Grant said. "they're not jittery. I live in a beach house myself and I know that nobody in our neighborhood has thought about moving out." He asked to be excused so he could prepare for the stage. Grant had been trying all through the trip to get people to send him copies of movie films taken, for his own collection. He would actually have people with the tour walk up to any amateur home movie camera owners and give them a contact number so he could pay for copies. When he heard that Iowa News Flashes, a local newsreel company, had been shooting the parade he said: "Wow! Tell him (the photographer) to send me a couple of dupes." He was so impressed with the Hollywood Victory Caravan experience, he told everyone who would listen that "these movies are going to be great, and I'll keep them for the rest of my life."

Bob Hope was greatly amused by a man backstage running around saying "Pst....Pst...." asking for quiet backstage. Each time he came by, Hope pointed him out, referring to him as the "pst-man."

When a reporter introduced himself to Groucho Marx, Marx rattled off about 15 minutes of wise cracks and insults. When he finished, he yelled for Bob Hope to "get over here, Hope! Give this newspaper man some of your best smart cracks!" When going over toward Hope, Grant, O'Brien, and Crosby, joined the group. They all agreed that doing the show was hectic, but Marx did not release the reporter yet. Marx stated that "This is a fugitive existence. We've had everything after us but the blood hounds. It's nice to be following the motor cycle cops, though. Usually they're chasing me!" Marx answered a question of what he uses when creating his mustache. "Anything I can get my hands on, including my wife's mascara!" he said, then added "It goes on a lot easier than it comes off!" Going toward the dressing room, Marx left the reporters by telling them that he hadn't seen so many people "since the bill collectors called on me in Beverly Hills!"

Merle Oberon expressed delight with being able to volunteer for the Caravan. "Everyone on this trip is so nice," she said. "With many of us in the same dressing rooms it could have very disagreeable with some nasty people in the group. But this group is marvelous. It's a funny thing you know, but most of us wouldn't think of going through what we've been through for money. I'm trying to see on this trip just how much the human body can stand. We'd all crab like the devil if we'd been hired to do this." Bob Hope kept a strict control of time, under the direction of Mark Sandrich. During the introduction, Bob Hope had a good reaction from the people of Des Moines. Within his first few sentences, he mis-pronounced the last letter of Des Moines. After a few references to his error, the audience seemed to forget and forgive him. Sharing the master of ceremonies duties with Cary Grant, and due to Hope's initial "Des Moines" mistake, Grant started speaking slowly whenever he used big words in dialogue with Hope.

Bert Lahr seemed consistently worried. He did not partake of the turkey sandwiches, shrimp, and salads set up for the cast. Instead he went out for a ham, egg and potato meal at the near-by Hotel Fort Des Moines. Other than him, most of the stars appeared nonchalant backstage. Frequently stars would be holding an conversation and hearing their cue, would excuse themselves and go out on stage. Several times Cary Grant went into a sound booth where he could don earphones so he could hear what Bob Hope was saying, for their word play on stage. Grant would laugh the whole time, as if he did not hear any of the jokes before. So much was ad-libbed that Grant had to be able to hear just to keep on an equal footing.

Joan Bennett was the only one on the train to travel with a dog - her pet poodle. Bennett quipped that when she returned to Hollywood she was going to have her dressing room done over into the size of a Pullman compartment and have all her clothes on something that swings back and forth. "I won't feel natural anymore, unless I do," she said.

Another old newspaper photo with Stan Laurel and Oliver Hardy filling out the drivers license application on stage at Shrine Auditorium.

An additional loud speaker system was borrowed and set up by W. F. Hartner of Indianola. He donated the loan of the equipment and eight additional microphones to ensure the entire show would be heard.

Old newspaper photo of Charlotte Greenwood and Pat O'Brien reviewing the script for their Des Moines appearance.

Bob Hope opened the show by mis-pronouncing Des Moines. After this error, for which he was forgiven, he told the story about the troupe's visit to the White House. After referring to it as "crowded", he went on to say that First Lady Eleanor flew in for the party, but Franklin was absent, "busy working on a spare tire."

Speaking with the starlets behind him, he mentioned working with such a beautiful group. He said "in Boston, I had drew a date who was at the original tea party. She was one of the bags they threw overboard."

Each star took their "shot" at Bob Hope. Joan Blondell asked Hope if many girls try to chase and grab him on the street. He responded with: "Oh, it's about even!" When he spoke of his "manly physique" he received remarks like "his mother must have been frightened by an avocado."

When introducing Bing Crosby, Hope stated that the man needed many pockets. "Bing doesn't pay an income tax. He just asks the government how much it needs this year. He has so much invested in his country that every time a Douglas bomber flies over his house it curtsies."

Cary Grant shared the hosting duties again. Claudette Colbert, Merle Oberon, and Joan Bennett kissed Grant as they came on stage. Hope told Grant that tonight he would "hide all of the actresses curling irons." Claudette responded with "If you're a Boy Scout, why do you try to kiss me?" Hope responded: "I belong to the Wolf patrol."

Charlotte Greenwood was the next act, and made sure she kissed Hope. Hope said "It had to be her, from the Boston Tea Party again!" and brought the house down.

When Pat O'Brien came on stage, he received a standing ovation that ran on and on. He walked up to the mike and said "Thank you. That was 90% for my wife, Eloise Taylor. She's from this town. I'll give her top billing tonight". That started the crowd roaring again.

Bing Crosby was singled out for his magenta pants and blue sports coat with brass buttons, as much as he was for his singing. All went as planned and Jimmy Cagney's numbers had the whole audience standing at the end of the show.

Since the travel distance was about 700 miles to their next city, the show ran without intermission and finished just after 6 PM. The stars were taken to the Rock Island Station by bus immediately after the show. It pulled out of the station before 8 PM.

DALLAS, TEXAS - May 11, 1942 - Arrival

The Hollywood Victory Caravan has a parade of stars on the afternoon of May 11th. Stan Laurel on the way from Union Station to their parade cars in Dallas, Texas.

Oliver Hardy heading to the car park, near the station, where the celebrity parade was starting.

Cary Grant waves to the greeting crowd.

Olivia de Havilland

Marie Mc Donald

Arlene Whelan

Charlotte Greenwood singing and dancing for the crowd.

Joan Blondell

Claudette Colbert

Charles Boyer.

Bing Crosby shares a laugh with a sailor.

Bing Crosby sitting in his parade car. All the stars used local drivers and convertibles.

Eleanor and "Mother" Powell.

Olivia de Havilland

Merle Oberon

Jimmy Cagney.

Jerry Colonna strikes a pose for the camera.

DALLAS, TEXAS - MAY 11, 1942

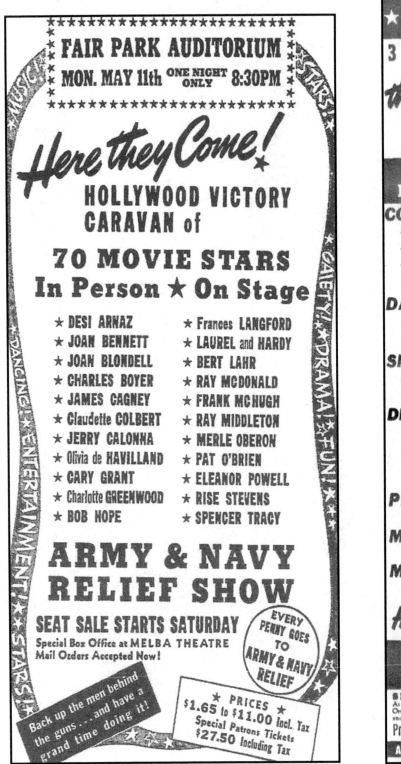

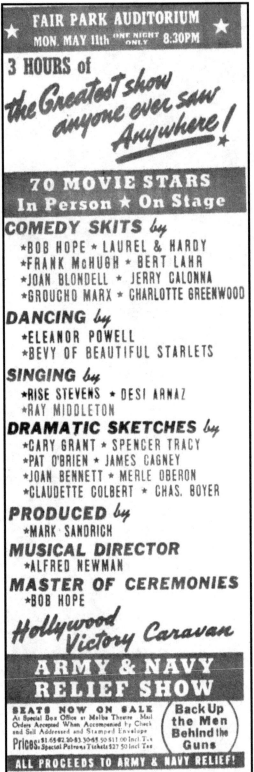

"The Greatest show anyone ever saw Anywhere!" Note Spencer Tracy still appears in some ads, even at this late date in the Caravan. An additional 350 "Standing Room" tickets were released for sale Monday morning at $2.20 each space.

Oliver Hardy and Bing Crosby pose at Union Terminal, in this old newspaper cutting.

Olivia de Havilland meets her escort Ensign Jack Crain at Union Station. Before he gets her autograph, she requests his.

Jerry Colonna watches as Merle Oberon responds to Bert Lahr's "best" Bela Lugosi impersonation when the train reaches Union Station.

Cary Grant was reunited with Lieutenant Alfred Delcambre of the US Navy at the Union Station. He won a Paramount search for talent contest, and under the name Del Cambre worked with Grant on the Paramount lot back in 1931-32. Photo shows Grant and Delcambre at the reception held at the Adolphus Hotel on Monday afternoon. From old newspaper clipping.

At the Dallas Union Station, the Star Spangled Special arrived at 2 PM, around 45 minutes late. The welcoming committee included Mayor Wordall Rogers and a 100 man honor guard of Army and Navy men who escorted the stars in 50 open cars to their hotels. Again hotel space was donated to the Caravan by both the Hotel Adolphus and Baker Hotels. The entire route from the station to Commerce street was jammed with fans. The crowds started forming before noon and did not break up until the last vehicle passed. It was at Commerce that the cars split up for their respective destinations, letting the stars enter in the main entrances to the hotels. The entrances to both the Baker and Hotel Adolphus were both packed and the police had difficulty clearing a pathway for the stars to reach the floors set aside for them.

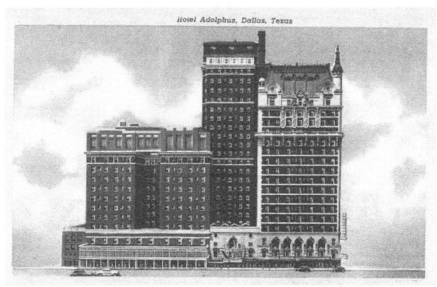

Hotel Adolphus from an old postcard as it appeared during the early 40's.

Baker Hotel from an old postcard as it appeared in the late 20's.

Once settled, both Merle Oberon and Bing Crosby immediately got out their golf clubs and went to nearby Brook Hollow for a quick game before that evening's performance, missing the 3 PM press conferences held in each hotel.

Following the press conferences, there was a war bond sale scheduled at Neiman-Marcus Department Store from 3:30 to 4:00. Neiman-Marcus had purchased $1500 worth of the $27.50 special patron tickets to be distributed to soldiers and sailors at nearby camps. An estimated fifteen thousand people jammed the store's entryways. No admission to the store was permitted without a purchase of a 25c war stamp. Sales stations were set up at all the store entrances.

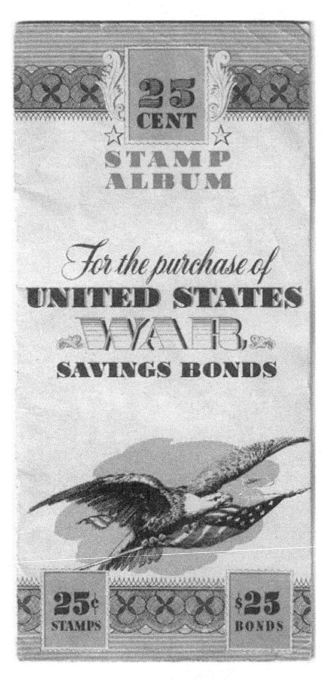

From the inside cover of the Stamp Album: "This Is Your Twenty-five Cent War Savings Stamp Album. Fill it with 75 Twenty-five Cent Stamps, and it will have a value of $18.75. Exchange it at the post office for a War Savings Bond which, after ten years will be worth $25.00. Then start filling another Stamp Album. War Savings Stamps are sold in five denominations - 10c, 25c, 50c, $1.00 and $5.00."

Some of the stars worked at Bond Sales counters that were conveniently located throughout the store. Participating were Cary Grant, Charles Boyer, Olivia de Havilland, Merle Oberon, Rise Stevens, Joan Bennett, Joan Blondell, Charlotte Greenwood, and Claudette Colbert. Bob Hope, also scheduled to appear in the store, had to dismiss himself due to his preparing for his radio broadcast, scheduled on Tuesday night. For the entire city, the only autographs available were with the purchase of War Bonds. Over 5000 people bought War Stamps to get into the store itself, bringing in over $1250. The first War Bond sale of the day was made by Joan Blondell, in the spacious Men's' Department. Mr. Marcus himself bought a $1000 War Bond and started the ball rolling.

One woman, was early in line buying her bond especially to get Charles Boyer's autograph. She bought her bond, and made her way away from the booth. After about 20 steps away, with her bond in her hand, she let out a yell. She turned and plowed back into the crowd with the force and speed of a professional football player. It took her just seconds to get back to Boyer's counter. "I forgot his autograph!" she shouted. "I'll get Boyer's autograph or else!" Charles Boyer not only gave her the autograph she forgot, but she also received a kiss on the cheek.

Charles Boyer signing autographs at his Neiman Marcus counter. Along with Cary Grant, their autographs were most in demand, and they sold the highest amount of bonds.

After a bit of rest after the daytime activities, a parade of open top cars took the performers from the two hotels to the Fair Park Auditorium for their 8:30 performance.

Groucho Marx in parade car. Without his stage make-up few recognize him. Here he grabs the hat of his escorting sailor and puts it on.

Members of the Dallas Career Girls organization have been actively participating behind the scenes during the entire Caravan's visit acted as ushers during the performance. They were also responsible for the set up of what was called "MacArthur's Bar" in the lobby to sell soft drinks, peanuts, popcorn, and programs in the lobby. The work by the Members added an additional $300 to the final total. Soft Drinks were 25c each, while ice water sold at $1.00 a glass. There was no intermission during that evening's show.

Between acts, Merle Oberon sold two all-star autographed programs, each one with a "kiss". The first program went to J. G. Parker of Fort Worth and sold for $500. The second program sold to R. J. O'Donnell, the Caravan's chairman for Dallas. His bid for this was $400.00. Adding this $900 brought the Dallas total up to $37,222, exceeding their goal by $2000.

The front of the Fair Park Auditorium in Dallas, Texas, from an old linen post card.

From left to right are Elyse Knox, Juanita Stark, Bob Hope, Frances Gifford, and Alma Carroll on stage for the opening.

Following the show's performance, the stars and other personnel were whisked to their hotels, checked out swiftly, and were back to the Star Spangled Special train for a 3:00 AM departure for Houston, where they were doing their final performance Tuesday evening. Ticket sales totaled $36,000 in Dallas.

DALLAS, TEXAS - "To Bob"

Bob Hope's autographed copy of the Hollywood Victory Caravan program was from their appearance at Fair Park Auditorium. Each town' program was somewhat different than the other's.

The center of the program has the Caravan's credit page for this show. This is autographed by many of the participants, from the musical director Alfred Newman to the troupe's doctor, Dr. Irving Newman.

Frank McHugh's photo did not make it into this program, so he signed the center, just under Arthur Newman's inscription.

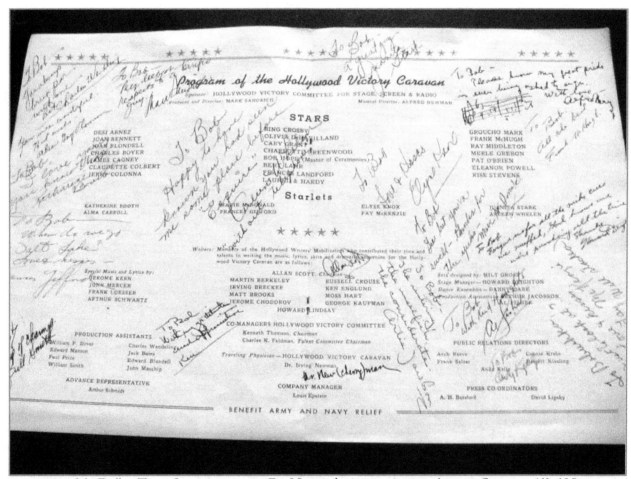

The center pages of the Dallas, Texas Souvenir program. Dr. Newman's signature is center, bottom. Composer Alfred Newman is in the upper right hand corner.

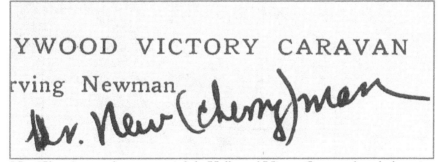

Dr. New(Cherry)man, who accompanied the Hollywood Victory Caravan through the entire tour.

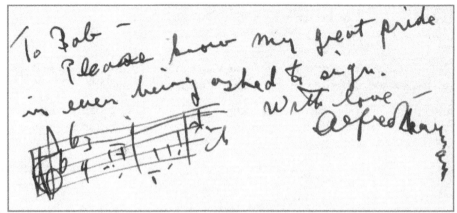

To Bob, Please know my great pride in even being asked to sign. With love --- Alfred Newman.

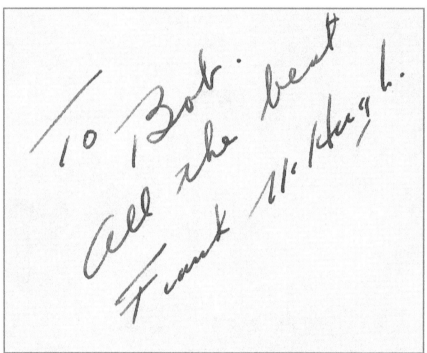

To Bob. All the best   Frank McHugh.

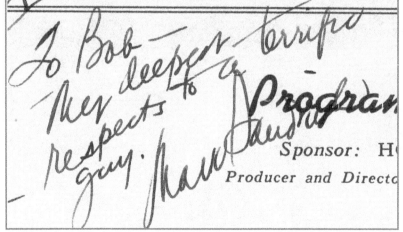

To Bob --- My deepest respects to a terrific guy. Mark Sandrich (Producer)

Charles Boyer

Dear Bob, It was really grand to make this trip with you - your fan, Charles "Beans" Boyer

To Bob --- It's great knowing you.   Rise

Bob: There is only one thing to say to you: "Thank you"   Desi
The photo is from the movie "Too Many Girls", filmed in 1940 with Ann Miller and Lucille Ball, (who were not on the Victory Caravan.

To Bob--- Hail, Straightman! Fondly, Cary

To "Hatchet Chin" from the Doll Boy   Bert Lahr

Joan Blondell

Where there's Hope there's life. See you in Huston Love Joan

To Bob --- I hope the Army and Navy realize what I did for them!   Love and hope   Claudette.

To Bob "Cassius" Hope from a friend ----- ----- ----- Jim

We all want to live with hope   *Joan*

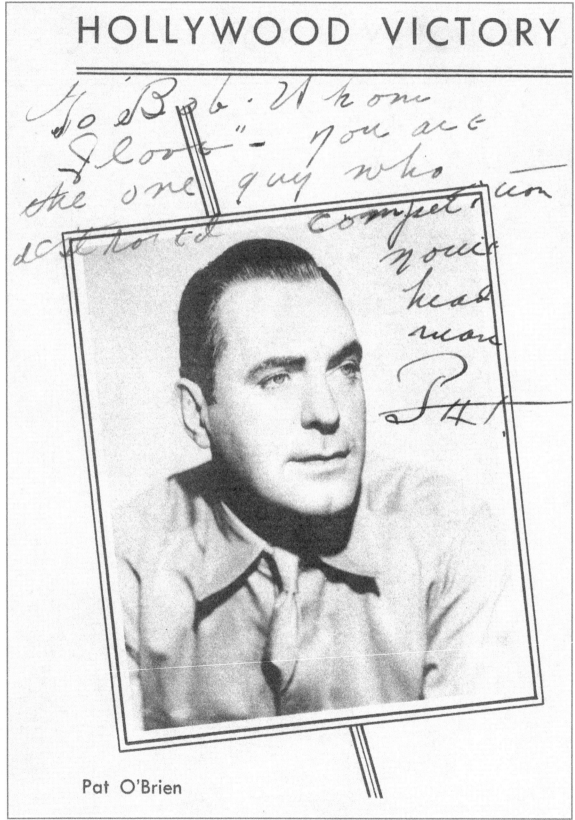

Pat O'Brien

To Bob --- Who I love--- you are the one guy who destroyed(?) competition   You're head man   Pat

Eleanor Powell

To "Bob" One in a million --- "Thanks for the Memory" It's a pleasure knowing you   Your friend Eleanor

To you "Bob" Thanks for the Memory   Stan & Babe
Oliver Hardy signed for himself and his partner, Stan Laurel.

To Bob with admiration and affection   Merle

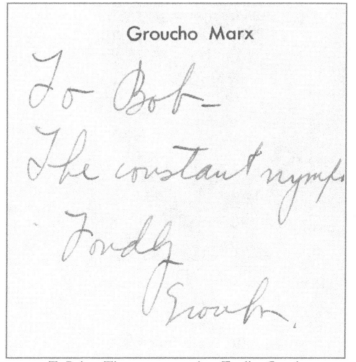

To Bob --- The constant nympho   Fondly   Groucho

To Bob in great admiration   Ray Middleton

Bob Darling. What a brake "I got" with my 'add' lib - Kiss -- Charlotte Greenwood

HOUSTON, TEXAS - May 12, 1942

Souvenir Program

HOLLYWOOD
Victory
CARAVAN

Presented for the benefit of the

ARMY EMERGENCY RELIEF
NAVY RELIEF SOCIETY

☆

COLISEUM
HOUSTON, TEXAS

☆

MAY 12, 1942

Inside page of the Houston Souvenir Program

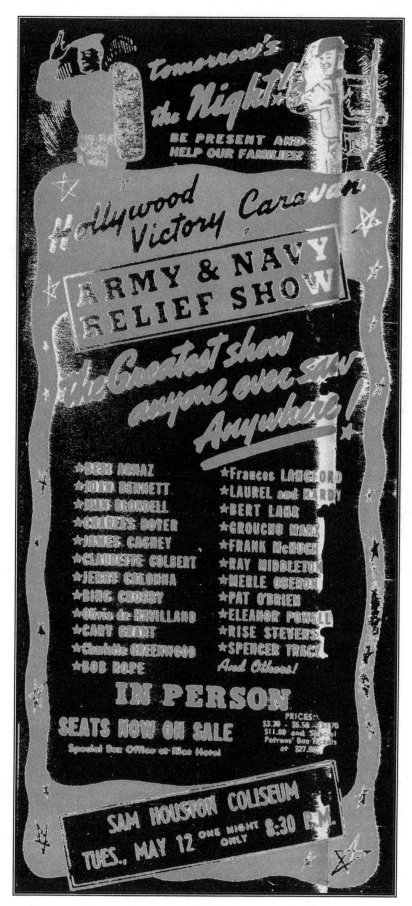

"Tomorrow's the Night - The Greatest show anyone ever saw Anywhere!"

From early in the morning a crowd had been gathered at the Rice Hotel, where the stars were staying in Houston, Texas. The Union Station was also packed when the "Star Spangled Special" arrived around 9:30 AM that Tuesday morning. Most of the performers stayed in their rooms on the train until just before show time. Some of the stars were spotted around town, however. Customers of Levy Brother's department store were surprised to see Joan Bennett on a shopping spree in what was to be the day of the final performance. Also seen on the street walking around were Jerry Colonna and Groucho Marx, out for some fresh air.

At high noon, a squadron of 24 planes from Ellington Field circled Houston in mass formation to salute the stars. The stars also had a contingent of soldiers and sailors protecting them from the fans during their stay here. No autographs were allowed, for security reasons, either at the station or the hotel. The stars were provided with jeeps for their transportation, and for the parade.

Rice Hotel, Houston, Texas.

Thousands of Houstonians were present at 7 PM when the parade formed on South Main Street. From there it proceeded from McGowan to Texas Avenue, then to Travis and Walker where the stars entered the coliseum for that night's performance. The Boy Scouts led the parade, carrying a large American flag horizontally, allowing the tossing of coins to land on its surface. More than $1000 in coin were gathered by the scouts, filling two large buckets. It took the Boy Scouts hours to count. Joan Blondell received the biggest reaction during the parade, since she was a native Texan.

More than 11,000 people saw that last performance, bringing in a total of $65,000. The ticket prices for the show in Houston were set at $5.50, $7.70, $11.00 and patron box seats at $27.50. The box office at the Texas Avenue entrance of the Rice Hotel remained open until tickets were sold. Every attendee received a fifty page deluxe souvenir program. This was the only city providing so large a book.

Exterior of the Sam Houston Coliseum, from an old linen postcard.

The packed interior of the Houston Coliseum minutes before the overture. While the quality of this surviving photo is not the best, visible in center is the art deco style stage set up for the evening. To either side of the stage (more visible on the right) is the large banner that reads: "MOTION PICTURE INDUSTRY   Hollywood Victory Caravan."

A badge worn by Officials at the final full cast Hollywood Victory Caravan.

After that evening's show, the entire cast boarded the train for Los Angeles. Like any other people working together, and having the same passion for their cause, a strong bond developed between the participants. According to Bert Lahr's son, John Lahr, one of Bert's largest memories of the ending of the tour was trying not to cry. Oliver Hardy, who Lahr described as outgoing and confident a funny man trying to look away from the group to hide his tears.

BOB HOPE'S RADIO BROADCAST - MAY 12, 1942

Bob Hope did not miss his radio broadcast on May 12. The Hollywood Victory Caravan performance went on as scheduled that evening at the Sam Houston Coliseum, and Bob Hope's first appearance on stage was 30 minutes into the show. The broadcast originated at the Music Hall which was adjacent to the Sam Houston Coliseum. The audience was made up of over 2700 student bombardiers from Ellington Field, in Houston. Mark Sandrich's unique form of direction allowed him to change the actor's order of appearance allowing Joan Bennett to appear on the show, along with Jerry Colonna and Francis Langford. Skinnay Ennis and his Orchestra along with Larry Keating rounded out the cast. The show was broadcast live on local WFAA and other NBC Stations.

Listing for May 12, 1942.

Jerry Colonna and Frances Langford wait off stage....

.....while Bob Hope is at the microphone.

SAN FRANCISCO, CALIFORNIA - May 19, 1942

Walter Winchell continued producing shows across the country for Navy relief. From his large show in Madison Square Garden, discussed in the second chapter, Winchell set up shows in many different cities. Despite the controversy surrounding Winchell himself over some of his political views, his popularity allowed him to leverage support for causes that he valued.

LIEUTENANT-COMMANDER WALTER WINCHELL WAS GREETED BY MAJOR HARRY MARTIN, OF THE U.S. ARMY MEDICAL STAFF ATTACHED TO LETTERMAN HOSPITAL, AT SAN FRANCISCO'S PRESIDIO HEADQUARTERS OF THE FOURTH ARMY COMMAND, FOLLOWING WINCHELL'S COAST-TO-COAST NEWS BROADCAST, THE FIRST TO COME FROM THE KGO-BLUE NETWORK STUDIOS AT SAN FRANCISCO'S NEW RADIO CITY. MAJOR MARTIN, WHOSE WIFE IS THE NOTED HOLLYWOOD COLUMNIST, LOUELLA PARSONS, IS AIDING NEW YORK'S COLUMNIST WINCHELL IN ARRANGEMENTS FOR THE PRESENCE OF MANY FILM AND MANY RADIO STARS ON THE HUGE U.S. NAVY RELIEF SHOW AT THE CIVIC AUD-ITORIUM, TUESDAY.

During the time that the Hollywood Victory Caravan was put together and performed, San Francisco was mentioned on and off as an additional city to visit. It never came to be part of the official tour stops, but eventually took place under the Hollywood Victory Caravan banner. While many of the stars of Caravan went back to prior commitments, a few of the Caravan members did one more show together in San Francisco, for Navy Relief., on the evening of May 19, 1942. A number of additional stars joined them, to replace the ones that left.

This last show did not get the response of the Caravan's original shows. Some of the critics of the day commented that the lack of management and planning for the show made it appear to be "tossed together," and "a poor shadow of the original."

Mark Sandrich was still the producer and director, but this program did not have any real rehearsal time. The lack of rehearsals and preparation for this night's appearance, and the removal of many of the dramatic sequences impacted the performers who were with the original tour. Morale for them was not the same with the different set of circumstances. On top of this, the newer talent were only doing a "one night performance". The "one for all and all for the show" was replaced with each act trying to be the "standout" for the evening.

The San Francisco Civic Auditorium, from an old linen postcard.

Critics referred to the San Francisco show as just being publicity for the stars involved, and thought the sketches were insipid instead of inspiring. The movie studios were not behind the artist for a single evening performance, as they had been through out. Cagney, Greenwood, and Lahr were no longer studio affiliated. Cantor and Jolson had ended their studio connections before the war. Without the studios, each star provided their own uniforms.

All along the prior journey the stars had been greeted by tumultuous crowds in each city. This not only made the stars and staff who were sacrificing their time for the cause feel welcome, but gave the people who could not afford a ticket a chance to be a part of the events. In San Francisco the stars did nothing between their noon arrival and the show time. Adding to the feeling of isolation, four hotels were used to house the troupe, separating the performers.

Even the official souvenir program was put together so rapidly, that the cast listing for the show differed with the photographs that were included. Included with the photos were Bob Hope, Jerry Colonna, and Frances Langford, who were doing a radio show that evening. Claudette Colbert and Olivia de Havilland were also pictured but were not in the cast that evening. It does not appear that either Bing Crosby or Spencer Tracy were a part of the show. Stan Laurel did appear with his partner, Oliver Hardy, but only Laurel's photo appeared in the program. Hardy's missing picture was never used.

Walter Winchell acted as the presenter of the program, and at various parts of the evening introduced the emcees Al Jolson and Eddie Cantor, who each performed a few songs, and Milton Berle who joked his way through the rest of the evening. Again, all appeared on the finale.

Although there were many citizens willing to volunteer to help with the event in both San Francisco and nearby Oakland, no use was made of them. There was no pre-publicity, press interviews or parades like in other cities, due to the one-shot nature of the show. No information of the arrival time of the train, or which stars would be on it was announced. Even the advertising for this city event was not impressive, with billboards calling the show "Walter Winchell's Hollywood Victory Caravan." The show was a sellout, taking in over $11,000 in ticket sales.

The Andrew Sisters brought in the biggest applause for the evening with "Boogie Woogie Bugle Boy," "Apple Blossom Time," and "You're a Lucky Fellow, Mr. Smith," from the hit movie "Buck Privates" with Abbott and Costello (1941). Lou Costello came out on stage for this number and clowned a bit as the Andrew Sisters left the stage and Bud Abbott came out to join him for "Who's On First?." Dinah Shore also did well. Singers had a bit of an advantage, since songs sung included many patriotic lyrics. Contemporary reviewers also stated that Laurel and Hardy did well with their Driver's License sketch. Cagney reprised his ending, and left everyone feeling that America's efforts would defeat the enemy. Winchell stated in his newspaper column the day following the show that the show "packed them in like sardines" and said that they could have sold another 20,000 tickets.

An announcement was made in Variety, the entertainment trade paper that on May 20th over 15,000 theaters would start a collection drive to add to the caravan's total. Twentieth Century Fox provided ads to be run in the theaters during the collections, which were done by ushers and theater staffs. Tyrone Power did the on-screen appeal, which took over 63,000 feet of raw film stock to make the distribution prints. Joseph Schenck chaired the drive, and used most of the same personal in an earlier March of Dimes drive which raised over 1.4 million.

Laurel and Hardy went over well with their Driver's License sketch, as did Abbott and Costello's "Who's on First." The Andrew Sisters brought in the biggest applause for the evening. Dinah Shore also did well. Singers had a bit of an advantage, since songs sung included many patriotic lyrics. Cagney reprised his ending, and left everyone feeling that America's efforts would defeat the enemy. Winchell stated in his newspaper column the day following the show that the show "packed them in like sardines" and said that they could have sold another 20,000 tickets.

Although no photos seem to exist of the stage performance in San Francisco, these photos of Laurel and Hardy on stage performing their Driver's License Sketch were taken in Dayton, Ohio by Robert Raetz in January, 1942.

Robert Raetz was a serviceman on leave when he took these photos with his 35mm still camera. (From the original negatives, courtesy of Robert Raetz.

IN THE END.......

An announcement was made in Variety, the entertainment trade paper that on May 20th over 15,000 theaters would start a collection drive to add to the caravan's total. Twentieth Century Fox provided ads to be run in the theaters during the collections, which were done by ushers and theater staffs. Tyrone Power did the on-screen appeal, which took over 63,000 feet of raw film stock to make the distribution prints. Joseph Schenck chaired the drive, and used most of the same personal in an earlier March of Dimes drive which raised over 1.4 million.

There was plenty of comment after the shows finished about the possibility of bringing the cast together for a film version that would be circulated to theaters. Were that done, army-navy relief might have made more than it did. Sadly, apart from a few home movies, no film record is known to exist of the Hollywood Victory Caravan

A short film after the war was made by Paramount. Called "The Hollywood Victory Caravan," it was made to sell Victory Bonds for the Treasury department. The film's only connection to the Army-Navy Relief effort was the presence of Bob Hope and Bing Crosby. While income raised by this film did not go directly into the relief funds, the money (now called Victory Bonds) helped to bring closure to our presence in other countries and bring back our military.

Certainly no picture with its array of talent ever has been made during the war years. While bond shows continued to be assembled and used for fundraising, none ever had this amount of talent, or reached as many of our citizens. This was our Greatest Generation, pulling together, sharing the sacrifices, and saving the freedoms that we all enjoy today.

The opening title of Paramount's 1945 war bond short, from a frame enlargement.

Original 1942 wooden plaque from a theater ticket booth advising patrons to support their country.

I. Joseph Hyatt is an entertainment archeologist. A member of the Sons of the Desert, the Laurel and Hardy Appreciation Society, Hyatt's articles have been printed internationally. Traveling across the US, and drawing on many collections, including his own, he brings back past eras with words and photographs.

His first book, "Stan Laurel's Valet - The Jimmy Murphy Story" was based on his close friendship with Jimmy Murphy. While a biography of one of the world's most entertaining valets, it's focus includes the 1940-42 US theatrical tours of Laurel and Hardy.

CPSIA information can be obtained
at www.ICGtesting.com
Printed in the USA
LVHW062054230522
719449LV00022B/406